Clear Thinking When Drinking

The Handbook for Responsible Alcohol Consumption

Roman T. Solohub

D0483335

Empennage Press
ACWORTH, GEORGIA

Although the author and publisher have made every effort to ensure the accuracy and completeness of information contained in this book, we assume no responsibility for errors, inaccuracies, omissions, or any inconsistency herein. Any slighting of people, places, or organizations is unintentional.

First printing 2007
ISBN-13: 978-0-9785719-0-0
ISBN-10: 0-9785719-0-8
LCCN: 2006904541

ATTENTION CORPORATIONS, UNIVERSITIES, COLLEGES, AND PROFESSIONAL ORGANIZATIONS: Quantity discounts are available on bulk purchases of this book for educational, gift purposes, or as premiums for increasing magazine subscriptions or renewals. Special books or book excerpts can also be created to fit specific needs. For information, please contact Empennage Press, PO Box 801082, Acworth, GA 30101.

To Christina and Ryan,
my two favorite kids.

Also to my dad, Janek,
who I miss very much, and who
was a quiet and brave soul.

He would have done anything for me.

CONTENTS

Chapter 9
Working for a Living

FOREWORD

If you're looking for a practical, no-nonsense, user-friendly guide to drinking in moderation, look no further. You're holding the right book.

People in our society are constantly bombarded with conflicting beliefs about alcoholic beverages:

- Alcohol is a poison
- Alcohol is the key to good health

- Alcohol is a drug that ensnares its victims
- Alcohol is a harmless social lubricant

- Alcohol leads to degradation and unhappiness
- Alcohol is essential to the good life

- Alcohol destroys brain cells
- Alcohol prevents Alzheimer's disease

- One drink of alcohol is the first step toward alcoholism
- Alcoholics aren't made but are born

What can we believe? This nontechnical but science-based book cuts through the dogma and prejudices to reveal what everyone needs to know about the consumption of alcoholic beverages—and how to avoid immoderate drinking. So let's drink a toast to the author. He and his book could change your life for the better.

—Dr. David Hanson

PREFACE

"One needs to recognize that it is not alcohol itself but rather the abuse of alcohol that is the problem."

(Hanson, 2001)

This is an ideal book for parents to give to their college-aged children or businesses to give to their employees. This book is also valuable as a reference for adults currently using alcohol who also may have some misconceptions about its properties. It's actually for anyone who decides to drink alcohol. It is not intended to encourage drinking. It is meant to discourage irresponsible, dangerous drinking. It also is not meant to discourage sensible consumption. There is a marked difference. The former can most definitely ruin your life; the latter can enhance it. You have to make the choice, and remember, *it is* a choice. You can follow the correct path down this varied road of choices with knowledge. This book, if given a chance, will impart you with that requisite knowledge. It is meant to empower anyone who makes the decision to drink with the required information to do so responsibly. Too many new college students ruin their lives, or at the least develop bad habits and misconceptions about alcohol use. These habits and misconceptions can lead to much more severe problems in the future.

Teaching responsibility toward alcohol doesn't require that young people consume alcohol any more than teaching them sex education requires them to have sex. Associating responsible consumption education with *enabling* underage drinking is a tremendous misconception. Lack of education *enables* inappropriate and dangerous drinking behaviors that put us all in danger. There is no intention here to encourage underage alcohol consumption; there is every intention to demand that anyone who chooses to drink, learn to do so responsibly

Alcohol is a powerful drug. It's the oldest and most widely used drug in the world. If you choose to use this legal drug—depending on age and when it's consumed, of course—learn what to expect. Everyone has his or her own limit. This book will teach you how to determine your own safe limits and enable you to enjoy the moderate consumption of alcohol.

ACKNOWLEDGMENTS

As with most projects, this book was made better through the input of others. For his kind contributions, my sincerest thanks go out to Dr. David J. Hanson, who wrote the Foreword to my book. Dr. Hanson was the source for many of the excerpts and information used in the book that greatly helped in getting the point across. His website, Alcohol Problems and Solutions (www.alcohol information.org) is an invaluable resource for anyone doing research on the topic of alcohol and its effects on society.

Thanks also go out to Dr. Dwight Heath for his article *Teach Safe Drinking to Your College-Bound Teen,* and to Dr. Ruth Engs for her interview with Dr. Hanson, *The Drinking Age Should Be Lowered.*

Several of the ideas in the book were highlighted with information from the works of Dr Gene Ford. One particularly excellent source is *The French Paradox and Drinking for Health.* I'm sorry to say that Dr. Ford passed away several months ago. Cheers to you, sir.

I'd also like to thank my friends who always stayed interested and kept me motivated to finish this project, especially Larry Sultze, who helped edit the book, John "Biff" Masciola, for his overall design expertise, and Jim and Donna Wensink, whose tangible item of encouragement sits upon my desk.

Finally, and most importantly, to my wife and best friend, Jennifer, who has stuck by me for more than 27 years. She edited and suggested and encouraged this book to completion; when she said it was ready, I knew it was.

INTRODUCTION

While sitting through college orientation with my daughter, it became painfully obvious that the university was expending a lot of energy and money warning of the ills of underage alcohol use. The various counselors and deans of different departments warned the students about the difficulties they would encounter if they drank. University policy on alcohol use in the dorms was revealed. The statistics on how alcohol affects the dropout rate and how it can damage the grade point average was discussed. The students even performed a skit to emphasize the hazards of alcohol.

Sitting through that same orientation two years later with my son indicated that apparently nothing had changed. Many and varied statistics were still being disseminated on the dangers of alcohol. Years ago, I heard the same message at my own orientation: Don't drink; we know you're going to drink but don't drink. I ignored that message way back when, my daughter ignored the message two years ago, and I'm quite sure my son is ignoring that same message now.

The drinking age in all 50 states is 21. This is not a federally set limit; the states can set their own standards, but if they deviate from this age limit, they lose federal funding, and for now, none of the states is willing to do so. It's likely the drinking age will remain 21. What does that mean? Well, for one thing, unless you delay going to college for a few years, you'll be too young to drink until your junior or possibly senior year. That settles that; no drinking. Case closed. No problem.

"College towns have college students, and college students drink," says Ingham County (Michigan) Commissioner Mark Grebner, who was a student at Michigan State University during the seventies. "People have got to come to grips with the fact that students are going to drink." This is the reality. Everyone knows college students are going to drink, and their parents pray they don't hurt themselves doing it. They hope their child is not the one passed out in the corner or the one with the lampshade on their head. They hope their child is not the one who wakes up in someone's front yard with no memory of how he or she got there. And even more, they hope their child doesn't get behind the wheel of a car after having those beverages that only a 21-year-old can have.

The orientations I sat through also made something else alarmingly obvious: Even though the consumption of alcohol by students was acknowledged, the correct and safe protocol of this consumption was not addressed; there was no class called Drinking 101. There are classes for virtually everything else—tennis, badminton, yoga, basket-weaving, and even the analysis of pornographic film (not my kids!). So why not responsible consumption? We've been teaching our children sex education from a young age, not because we were encouraging sex, but because we know that empowering them with the knowledge of how to have sex safely was much better than the alternative. Being sexually active in ignorance is not bliss; it is dangerous. The misuse of alcohol through ignorance is at least as dangerous.

Some experts agree.

Teach Safe Drinking to Your College-Bound Teen
by Dwight B. Heath, Ph.D.

It once was a unanimously happy occasion when a high school senior was accepted at the college of his or her choice. But that enthusiasm has been dampened somewhat by reports of sexual assault, rape, violence, and deaths associated with binge drinking on college campuses.

We could blame the media for sensationalizing these stories. Or we could blame the universities, or society as a whole. But none of this will mask the grim reality that too many college students drink too much, and there are serious risks involved in their doing so.

What are you, as a parent of a college-aged student, to do? It may be tempting to warn students about the dangers of drinking, but most adolescents already have heard most of the warnings and even may have seen some of the consequences. A majority already have done some experimenting on their own.

Current research holds that more than half of high school seniors in this country already drink more than once a month. Even if they are not binging, they know from the experience of others that it rarely appears to have lasting consequences. For many teens, the risks can seem to be exaggerated, and the pleasures of drinking certainly are not discussed in health class.

They also know that soon they will have easy access to beer and other alcoholic beverages (even if they haven't until now) and will face considerable peer pressure to "be sociable," "relax," and "have fun."

Anyone who cares about an aspiring college student should respect that person enough to talk frankly about the risks of excessive drinking, just as they would about the risks of using drugs or of careless spending.

As a parent and longtime member of a university community familiar with drinking problems in many countries, I am convinced that most young people should learn both how to drink, and how not to drink—whether that means declining a drink, avoiding certain places or people, or simply holding a glass for a long time.

For many adults, it can be fun to drink in moderation —with food, with talk, with no intention of getting drunk. There is a rapidly growing body of research that indicates that moderate drinkers (about two drinks per day for males, one drink per day for females) are at less risk for developing cardiovascular disease and have lower death rates from many causes, compared both to nondrinkers and heavy drinkers.

People don't have to drink if they don't want to. We know that individuals vary enormously in their responses to alcohol, and some people should not drink at all. However, college students will have to make the decision for themselves each time they find themselves in a situation where alcohol is available. They will have to make this decision based on their own knowledge, experiences, and wants. In light of this, it is critical that parents or guardians equip their college-bound students with some realistic, practical guidelines. I suggest the following:

- Never drink just for the sake of drinking, as a game or contest, or with the aim of getting drunk or forgetting troubles.
- Don't drink on an empty stomach. Eat both before and while drinking.
- Pace yourself. Until you are familiar with your own reactions to alcohol, don't consume more than one drink per hour. One drink can be a 12-ounce can or bottle of beer, a 4-ounce glass of wine, or 1 ounce of liquor in a mixed drink. Remember that carbonated drinks get alcohol into the bloodstream faster.
- Know when to say "when." Monitor your own feelings. Be wary of any changes in mood or perceptions.

Yes, I know that it is illegal in all 50 states to sell alcoholic beverages to anyone under 21. Although most college officials do not ignore the law openly, neither do they enforce it very vigorously.

Throughout our history, there has been a love-hate relationship with drink, and it seems unfair to send students off to college without at least some basic guidelines. A few simple precautions may help even the best students to enjoy and benefit more fully from all aspects of their experiences at college.

*Reprinted with permission of the author and publisher, from "Teach Safe Drinking to Your College-Bound Teen," *The Addiction Letter,* vol. 11, no. 8, unpaginated special insert, 1995.

Dr. Dwight Heath, *a graduate of Yale and Harvard, is Professor Emeritus of Anthropology at Brown University and is the world's leading anthropological authority on drinking. He is an adviser on alcohol to a broad range of national and international organizations and recently edited the* International Handbook on Alcohol and Culture.

It's Better to Teach Safe Use of Alcohol
by David J. Hanson, Ph.D.

Many societies and groups have successfully prevented alcohol problems. How can we apply their techniques both in our families and in our society to reduce the abuse of beer, wine, and distilled spirits or liquor?

With much wringing of hands, we seem to be a nation petrified by the thought that someone somewhere may be drinking too much and running amok. Many activists feed this paranoia with their insistence on talking about alcohol in the same breath as illicit drugs.

And yet, humankind has had a relationship with beverage alcohol for over 6,000 years, suggesting that we need to divorce the subject from the emotionalism that has engulfed it, and approach it from a more intelligent, reasonable perspective.

Abusive drinking is, without question, a serious problem. But we will never make real progress against that problem until we take a hard look at the approach modeled by those cultures that have established a "truce" with alcohol—from Italians to Greeks to Jews to many others.

And what exactly is the model these cultures share? It can be defined on three levels:

Beliefs About the Substance of Alcohol—In these cultures, the substance of alcohol is seen neutrally. It is neither a terrible poison nor a magic potion.

The Act of Drinking—The act of drinking is seen as natural and normal. At the same time, there is little or no social pressure to drink, and absolutely no tolerance for abusive drinking.

Education About Drinking—Education about drinking starts early and starts in the home. Young people are taught—under their parents' supervision, through their parents' example—that if they drink, they should drink moderately.

To date, this three-part approach has allowed many cultures to avoid the alcohol abuse problems plaguing our society. Still our federal government and many others in the U.S. prevention field fail to learn from this model—opting instead to depict alcohol as a "dirty drug," something to be shunned and feared; to promote abstinence as the best choice for all people; to work toward reducing all drinking.

Contrasting alcohol "policy" in our culture with the policies promoted elsewhere, we are presented with several logical steps:

1. Encourage moderate use of alcohol among those who choose to drink. Moderate drinking and abstinence should be presented as equally acceptable choices. Those who choose to drink should not force drinking upon abstainers. Those who choose not to drink should have comparable respect for those who do.

2. Make systematic efforts to clarify and promote the distinctions between acceptable and unacceptable drinking. Effective education is based on much more than telling people what not to do.

3. Firmly penalize unacceptable drinking, both legally and socially. While the criminal justice system has an important role to play in this effort, the most essential role is played by individual peers. Intoxication must never be humored and never accepted as an excuse for "bad behavior."

4. End the current reduction-of-consumption approach to dealing with alcohol abuse. This approach wrongly assumes that the substance of alcohol is the necessary and sufficient cause of all drinking problems and that the availability of alcohol determines the extent to which it will be consumed and abused. Accordingly, policies developed from this approach focus on limiting (or reducing) availability. And because they are founded on questionable assumptions, such policies not only fail to achieve their objectives; they may, in fact, be counterproductive, especially when we consider the evidence suggesting that moderate drinking can enhance individual health.

5. Finally, end all attempts to stigmatize beverage alcohol as a "dirty drug," as a poison, as inherently harmful. Demonizing alcohol serves no practical purpose, contributes to cultural emotionalism and ambivalence, and exacerbates the problems it seeks to solve.

Reasonable people, reasonably concerned about these issues, should give this proven approach a chance. If so, America will surely place itself on course toward a far more successful relationship with the beverage alcohol.

---

*Reprinted from Alcohol Problems and Solutions (www.alcoholinformation.org) by permission of the author.

Dr. David J. Hanson, Ph.D., is Professor Emeritus of Sociology at the State University of New York at Potsdam. Professor Hanson has researched the subject of alcohol and drinking for over 30 years, beginning with his Ph.D. dissertation investigation. Shortly thereafter, he began a continuing series of nationwide studies of collegiate drinking over time (since 1981 with Dr. Ruth C. Engs of Indiana University). He has received alcohol research grants from federal and state agencies, published over a dozen chapters in books on alcohol, prepared articles for several encyclopedias, *and recently published two books on alcohol. His publications and scholarly papers number over 300 and textbooks in over a dozen fields of study report his research. Dr. Hanson has served as alcohol consultant to the Canadian government and testified on Capitol Hill; his research has repeatedly been reported in the* New York Times *and other major newspapers, where he is frequently quoted; and he has appeared as an alcohol expert on the* NBC Nightly News *with Tom Brokaw, the BBC's* The World Tonight, *the* Dr. Laura *television program, the Fox News Channel, CNN Saturday, National Public Radio's* All Things Considered, To the Best of Our Knowledge, *the ABC national radio news, and more than 60 radio programs across the country.*

I agree with doctors Heath and Hanson. I thought that since most young people were likely to try alcohol, it would be better they be taught how to use it safely rather than just winging it. In other words, if we make the assumption that alcohol consumption is a learned behavior, like just about everything else we do, why not have a reference to learn from? Please don't misunderstand; I'm not encouraging drinking, I'm just trying to be realistic. This issue has been pertinent for many generations, and I have yet to find a definitive source document that provides the necessary guidelines about responsible consumption.

I wish I had been provided with some sort of guidelines when I attended college. If college drinking today is anything like it was back then, the term guzzling would better describe the activity. I shudder when I think about just how much we would drink, guzzle, chug, and much too often get sick. We never counted our drinks. We drank until we were done, and we were done when we stopped drinking; it was that simple. We only kept track of how many drinks we consumed if we were trying to out-drink each other. If someone were to ask how much I drank the night before, I'd have no idea. We needed guidance, but we had none.

This handbook is designed to provide those guidelines. It also contains facts about alcohol and its effects on the human body that are important to understand if you decide to drink. Remember, there is no requirement that you drink. Millions of people get by every day without consuming alcohol. It may not be for you, and that's great! But if you are like the majority of people, you're at least going to try alcohol at some time during your life.

This handbook can help you to better understand what to expect if you decide to use alcohol, and is intended to empower the reader with the practical, factual knowledge required to drink responsibly.

CHAPTER 1

Alcohol...Friend or Foe

Alcohol for consumption has been around, in some estimates, since the Neolithic Period about 10,000 years ago. Before that, animals feasting on naturally fermented fruits were probably the first to experience the effects of mild intoxication. Stone Age man might have tasted the interesting flavor of naturally fermented honey and enjoyed it. No doubt it was just a matter of time before they let that honey age purposely and produced the first honey wines or meads. The development of agriculture about 6,000 years ago led to the development of beer, and then later, wine. Alcoholic beverages were an important staple in Western civilization, supplying fluids when the water supplies were tainted and calories when food was scarce. In fact, until about the last hundred years or so, alcohol in one form or another, had been the most popular daily drink for the last 5,000 years.

There are many different types of alcohol. The type we drink is ethyl alcohol or ethanol (CH_3CH_2OH). What we drink is not pure alcohol but a beverage containing diluted alcohol. Alcoholic beverages include wines, beers, and liquor or distilled spirits. Alcohol is produced during a natural process called fermentation, which occurs when yeast, a microscopic fungus, reacts with carbohydrates. This releases an enzyme called zymase, which creates alcohol and releases carbon dioxide. This process continues until the concentration of alcohol reaches a natural level of 11 to 14 percent, at which point most strains of yeast die, literally producing alcohol to the point of destroying themselves. Wine is fermented from the sugars in fruits or berries, with grapes being the most common choice. Wine can also be produced from various plants or their saps, from honey, and even from milk.

As mentioned, because most strains of yeast cannot tolerate alcohol concentrations much above 14 percent, most naturally fermented wines contain between 11 and 14 percent alcohol. Beers are fermented from grains after the starch in them is converted to sugar. In beer, the alcohol content varies from about 2 percent in some mild varieties, up to more than 14 percent in especially strong Belgian ales and malt liquors. American craft beer, a category in which you find some of the world's most meticulously brewed and best-tasting varieties, runs the gamut from 2 percent to beyond 20 percent in some instances. Most commercial beers brewed in the United States contain between 4 and 7 percent alcohol.

Distillation is the process used to make beverages with higher alcohol content, such as whiskey. In this process the fermented liquid is heated until it vaporizes, the vapor is then cooled until it condenses back into a liquid form. These distilled "spirits" contain between 40 and 50 percent alcohol.

Proof is the alcohol industry's method of indicating strength or concentration. Bootleggers and early distillers would "prove" the purity of their liquor by submitting it to flame testing. Buyers would try to ignite a spoonful of the beverage; if it sustained a flame it was "proven" to be of sufficient concentration. The term, which has stuck throughout the years, is simply two times the percentage by volume; so a bottle of vodka that is 80 proof, is 40 percent alcohol by volume; a bottle of wine that is 24 proof is 12 percent by volume, and so on. The higher the proof, the more potent the beverage.

Once again, the alcohol in these drinks is ethyl alcohol, but there are small amounts of other alcohols, such as amyl, butyl, propyl, and methyl alcohol, which occur as byproducts of fermentation. These biologically active compounds are called congeners and are thought to contribute to the dreaded hangover. Congeners also include acids, aldehydes, esters, ketones, phenols, and tannins; there are also numerous inorganic substances, including vitamins and minerals. Some of these ingredients are derived from primary plant materials. Others are produced during the fermentation process and may be reduced by purification. Still others are introduced during the aging process, such as the continuous contact with oak barrels during the aging of various whiskies. Congeners contribute special characteristics of taste, aroma, and color to the beverages. Some have toxic effects, and depending on their concentrations, can interfere with the metabolism of alcohol. These impurities usually lend color to the liquid so the clearer the drink, usually the fewer congeners it contains.

To understand alcohol's effect on the human body (and mind), it is important to understand how it is absorbed. There is no requirement for alcohol to be digested before it begins its work. Alcohol is absorbed directly into the bloodstream and quickly finds its way to your brain. A drink—whether a beer, glass of wine, or shot—starts being absorbed as soon as it comes in contact with the lining of the mouth and esophagus. It enters the stomach, where more of it is absorbed, then it goes through the pylorus and enters the small intestine, where the majority is absorbed. About 5 percent is absorbed in the mouth and esophagus, about 20 percent in the stomach, and the remaining 75 percent through the small intestine where it quickly enters the bloodstream and circulates with the blood throughout the body. Once in the bloodstream, alcohol finds its way to the brain and the drinker feels its effect. The quicker it gets into the small intestine and the bloodstream, the quicker the effect it has on the individual.

Although alcohol is metabolized or broken down primarily in the liver, the body begins to dispose of alcohol immediately after it has been absorbed. An insignificantly small proportion of alcohol is exhaled through the lungs, and a tiny amount is excreted in sweat. A small level is secreted by the kidneys and will be accumulated and retained in the bladder until eliminated in the urine. Only 2 to 10 percent of the alcohol is eliminated by these means.

The remainder, 90 percent or more of the absorbed alcohol, is disposed of in the liver. As alcohol is passed through the liver by the circulating blood, it is acted upon by alcohol dehydrogenase (ADH), a zinc-containing enzyme found chiefly in the liver cells. The alcohol is converted by this process to acetaldehyde, itself a highly toxic substance, but this is immediately acted upon by acetaldehyde dehydrogenase, another enzyme, and converted to acetate, carbon dioxide, and water. A coenzyme called nicotinamide adinine dinucleotide (NAD) is also involved and seems to be the limiting factor in the rate of alcohol metabolism. This rate of alcohol metabolism is about a half ounce of pure alcohol per hour in an average-sized man. This is the equivalent of one 12-ounce beer, 5 ounces of wine, or one shot of 80-proof liquor. Alcohol releases about 200 calories per ounce during this oxidation process, so alcohol releases energy during its metabolism but has no nutritional value.

The limit on the rate at which the body can dispose of alcohol results in its accumulation in the body if drinking proceeds at a faster rate than the alcohol is metabolized. So if you drink at a rate that exceeds the rate at which the body can metabolize the alcohol, your blood alcohol level will go up.

The level of absorption in the body is reflected in the blood alcohol level (BAL), or blood alcohol concentration (BAC). These terms simply indicate the measured amount of alcohol present in the blood. A BAC of 0.10 means that a person has 1 part alcohol per 1,000 parts of blood in the body. These measurements of blood alcohol levels are what the various states use to set the "legal limits" for drinking and driving.

Many things affect the rate of absorption. Size, body weight, gender, and quantity consumed all have an effect. The rate of consumption and whether or not you drink on an empty stomach also have a tremendous effect. The key to understanding how blood alcohol concentrations are affected is to think of the body as a container; the bigger the container, the more fluid it contains, and the more fluid it contains, the more it can dilute the alcohol put into it. A 150-pound man has less fluid in his body than a 250-pound man, so the smaller man will see a rise in his BAC much more quickly than the larger man.

Pound for pound, women are affected more by alcohol than men; that is, their BAC will increase more quickly than a man's. There are several reasons for this. Women tend to store more fat than men and alcohol does not dissolve readily in fat. Women also have a smaller amount of water present in their bodies to aid in the dilution of the alcohol. Women have less of the alcohol metabolizing enzyme ADH. The deficiency in these ADH levels slows down the metabolism or breakdown of the alcohol, thereby allowing the alcohol more time to remain in the body and increasing the BAC, which leads to a more rapid, longer lasting intoxication. As a man ages, however, his ADH levels go down until, at about age 50, the levels are about the same as those of a woman (Beyerlein 1999). This is one factor in explaining why a man's tolerance for alcohol declines as he gets older.

Drinking on an empty stomach significantly speeds up the rate of alcohol absorption. Just think about it: If your stomach is empty there's nothing to interfere with alcohol's progress to the small intestine. If, on the other hand, there is food in your stomach, two things happen. First, the pyloric sphincter closes, blocking the path to the small intestine and allowing the stomach time to digest the food; second, some of the alcohol is absorbed into the food itself, thereby slowing its progress to the small intestine even further. Since the body absorbs most of the alcohol through the small intestine, this delay results in a slower rise in blood alcohol level and slower rate of intoxication, depending on the rate of consumption.

Obviously, the more alcohol you introduce into your system, the more alcohol will get into your bloodstream and your brain, and the more intoxicated you'll become. How strong your drinks are—or how much alcohol they contain—along with the rate at which you drink them will have a direct effect on the level of intoxication you experience.

Not all drinks are created equally. We already know that whiskey and vodka are stronger, ounce for ounce, than wine, and wine is usually stronger than beer. It is important to determine how they compare in strength, under normal conditions of consumption. In general:

one beer = one glass of wine = one shot (1.5 ounces) of liquor

A 12-ounce beer, a 5-ounce glass of wine, and a 1.5-ounce shot of 80-proof liquor all contain about 0.6 oz. of pure alcohol. What you drink does not matter; what matters is how many ounces of this alcohol you consume, given the same amount of time. Obviously, you can consume shots more quickly than a glass of beer. A shot will affect you more rapidly and can get you into trouble if too many are consumed too quickly, but it is the quantity of pure alcohol that matters, not the fact that it's liquor. If consumed over the same amount of time, 10 glasses of wine will do the same damage as 10 beers or 10 drinks or 10 shots. Don't make the mistake of assuming that since beer is so mild a drink, it can't hurt you; it can and will if drunk to excess.

Questions

1. What type of alcohol do we drink?

2. What is proof?

3. What is stronger, a beverage that is 50 proof or one that is 20 percent alcohol by volume?

4. Does alcohol need to be digested in order to be absorbed?

5. Will the presence of food in your stomach affect the rate at which you absorb alcohol?

6. What is a drink?

CHAPTER 2

Trusted With a Gun But Not a Bottle

Everyone seems to have an opinion on the drinking age. Although this book discusses the appropriate means of responsible consumption and is not intended as a protest against or an endorsement for our government's restrictions, I think a short discussion on the matter is important.

The United States has the dubious distinction of setting the most stringent minimum age limit on alcohol consumption in the free world. Although the age 21 policy is not a federally mandated law, currently all states in the union have set 21 as the "magic age" of minimum consumption. The national Minimum Drinking Age Act of 1984 requires states to raise their minimum purchase and public possession age to 21. States that do not comply lose highway funds under the Federal Highway Aid Act. So the federal government, pressured by strong lobbying groups such as Mothers Against Drunk Drivers (MADD), in turn pressures the states with a gun to their heads called money. The states, not willing to part with their windfall, ignored the rights of their young adults and all raised the minimum drinking age to 21.

Now, admittedly, the idea behind the minimum drinking age is an honorable one; its proponents believe it saves lives. They believe it decreases the incidence of automobile accidents and fatalities. (I thought we already had laws that prohibit drinking and driving at any age.) I'm sure if we raised the drinking age to 31, we'd save even more lives. If we really wanted to impact automobile safety, we'd raise the driving age, although that wouldn't be practical because parents would have to drive their kids everywhere.

I find it difficult to accept the fact that our country can send our young men and women to foreign lands at the age of 18 to die for their country, and yet not allow those same young men and women, if they survive battle, to have a beer when they get back home. I think it ridiculous that young married couples, some of whom have children of their own, cannot have a glass of wine with dinner. Of all the civilized countries on earth, the United States has the most restrictive drinking age, and yet, the United States is also the country that suffers the most from the repercussions of underage drinking exactly because of those illogical policies.

The 21 and under demographic has no powerful lobbying group to represent them in Washington, so instead, they become the brunt of the ambivalent and unscientific policies of our government and our society. Take their rights away; they won't do anything about it. Let them vote, get married, drive heavy machinery, fly airplanes, get killed for their country, but God forbid they have a beer! Call them adults, expect them to be accountable for their actions, but make them hide in the back of an alley to chug their booze in a hurry before they get caught. Ignore the experts who actually use research to make the determination that the age 21 policy is counterproductive to responsible consumption. Ignore the examples set by Italy, Germany, Greece, and countless other countries that have much more reasonable laws, and yet have fewer problems with alcohol abuse. Set a standard that is illogical, just because you can. This is idiocy, but money and the stigma attached to alcohol use talks.

Here's an example of what the real experts have to say on the matter.

The Legal Drinking Age: Science Versus Ideology
by David J. Hanson, Ph.D.

Underlying minimum age legislation are the assumptions of American prohibitionism: Alcohol consumption is undesirable and dangerous. It typically results in problem behavior. Drinking in any degree is equally undesirable because moderate social drinking is the forerunner of chronic inebriation. Naturally, young people, if not everyone, should be protected from alcohol, according to this view. However, following the repeal of the Eighteenth Amendment in 1933, prohibition efforts have largely been age-specific. Although repeal abolished Prohibition in general, prohibitionists have tried to maintain their hold over young people. "The youngest age group is...chosen as a symbolic gesture because of its political impotence and because...there are not major economic consequences...." And there have been no political consequences; young people tend not to vote or otherwise hold politicians accountable for their actions.

Neo-prohibitionists of today typically argue that raising the drinking age to 21 has been beneficial. However, the evidence suggests a different story. For example, a study of a large sample of young people between the ages of 16 and 19 in Massachusetts and New York after Massachusetts raised its drinking age revealed that the average, self-reported daily alcohol consumption in Massachusetts did not decline in comparison with New York. Comparison of college students attending schools in states that had maintained, for a period of at least 10 years, a minimum drinking age of 21 with those in states that had similarly maintained minimum drinking ages below 21 revealed few differences in drinking problems. A study of all 50 states and the District of Columbia found "a positive relationship between the purchase age and single-vehicle fatalities." Thus, single-vehicle fatalities were found to be more frequent in those states with high purchase ages.

Comparisons of drinking before and after the passage of raised minimum age legislation have generally revealed little impact upon behavior. For example, a study that examined college students' drinking behavior before and after an increase in the minimum legal drinking age from 18 to 19 in New York State found the law to have no impact on underage students' consumption rates, intoxication, drinking attitudes, or drinking problems. These findings were corroborated by other researchers at a different college in the same state. A similar study at Texas A&M University examined the impact of an increase in consumption or alcohol problems among underage students. However, there was a significant increase among such students in attendance at events where alcohol was present. There were also significant increases in the frequency of their requests to legal-age students to provide alcohol and in their receipt of illicit alcohol from legal-age students.

A longitudinal study of the effect of a one-year increase of the drinking age in the province of Ontario found that it had a minimum effect on consumption among 18- and 19-year-old high school students and none among those who drank once a week or more. A similar study was conducted among college students in the State University System of Florida to examine their behavior before and after an increase in the drinking age from 19 to 21. While there was a general trend toward reduced consumption of alcohol after the change in law, alcohol-related problems increased significantly. Surveys at Arizona State University before and after that state raised the legal drinking age from 19 to 21 found no reduction in alcohol consumption. Finally, an examination of East Carolina University students' intentions regarding their behavior following passage of the 21-year-age drinking law revealed that only 6 percent intended to stop drinking, 70 percent planned to change their drinking location, 21 percent expected to use a false or borrowed identification to obtain alcohol, and 22 percent intended to use other drugs. Anecdotal statements by students indicated the belief of some that it "might be easier to hide a little pot in my room than a six pack of beer."

Over the past four decades it has been demonstrated that the proportion of collegiate drinkers increases with age. However, in July of 1987, the minimum purchase age became 21 in all states. Because drinking tends to be highly valued among collegians and because it is now illegal for those under 21 to purchase alcohol, Dr. Ruth Engs and I hypothesized that reactance motivation would be stimulated among such students, leading more of them to drink. The data from 3,375 students at 56 colleges across the country revealed that, after the legislation, significantly more underage students drank compared to those of legal age. Thus, the increase in purchase age appears to have been not only ineffective but actually counterproductive, at least in the short run.

The prohibitionists and their current neo-prohibitionists counterparts are clearly wrong in their assumptions. Drinking in moderation is neither undesirable nor dangerous but is actually associated with better health and greater longevity than is either abstention or heavy drinking. In short it is not bad but good and healthful. And drinking does not typically result in problem behavior. Similarly, moderate drinking is clearly not a forerunner of inebriation. To the contrary, the vast majority of drinkers enjoy the benefits of alcohol and never become problem drinkers.

People become responsible by being properly taught, given responsibility, and then held accountable for their actions. We don't tell young people to "just say no" to driving, fail to teach them to drive, and then on their 18th birthday give them drivers' licenses and turn them loose on the road. But this is the logic we follow for beverage alcohol because neo-prohibitionism underlies our alcohol policy.

Its time for our alcohol policy to be based on science rather than ideology.

---

*Reprinted from Alcohol Problems and Solutions (www.alcoholinformation.org) by permission of the author.

The Drinking Age Should Be Lowered
Interview with Dr. Ruth Engs, by Dr. David J. Hanson

The minimum drinking age continues to stir controversy, with recent proposals being made to reduce or qualify the minimum legal age at which drinking may occur. One of the more influential proponents of lowering the drinking age is Dr. Ruth Engs, professor of Applied Health Sciences at Indiana University in Bloomington.

Dr. Hanson: Dr. Engs, could you explain your proposal to lower the drinking age?

Dr. Engs: I'd be glad to. I propose that the drinking age be lowered to about 18 or 19 and permit those of legal age to consume in socially controlled environments such as restaurants and official school and university functions. Currently, we prohibit 20-year-olds from sipping champagne at their own weddings! I also propose that individuals of any age be permitted to consume alcohol under the direct supervision of their parents in their own homes.

Dr. Hanson: How would this be more effective than the 21 age laws?

Dr. Engs: Although the legal purchase age is 21, a majority of young people under this age consume alcohol, and too many of them do so in an irresponsible manner. This is largely because drinking is seen by these youth as an enticing "forbidden fruit," a "badge of rebellion against authority," and a symbol of adulthood. Our nation has twice tried prohibition, first at the state level in the 1850s and at the national level beginning in 1920. These efforts to prevent drinking were unenforceable and created serious social problems such as widespread disrespect for law, the growth of organized crime, and the development of immoderate consumption patterns.

The flaunting of the current age-specific prohibition is readily apparent among young people who, since the increase in the minimum legal drinking age, have tended to drink in a more abusive manner than do those of legal age. This, of course, is exactly what happened in the general public during national Prohibition.

Dr. Hanson: So raising the legal drinking age has made things worse?

Dr. Engs: Yes. Like national Prohibition, it has been counterproductive. Raising the drinking age was much worse than doing nothing.

Dr. Hanson: But hasn't drinking been going down among young people?

Dr. Engs: Yes, the proportion of the American population who drink (including young people) has been going down since about 1980. That was long before the states were required to raise the drinking age in 1987. And of course legislation wouldn't have limited consumption among those aged 21 or older.

On the other hand, while fewer young people are drinking and their average consumption levels have been dropping (along with that of the general population), more younger people tend to drink abusively when they do consume. This change occurred after the increase in the drinking age.

Dr. Hanson: So, it's a little like what happened during national Prohibition?

Dr. Engs: Exactly. Prohibition tended to destroy moderation and instead promoted great excess and abusive drinking. People tended to gulp alcohol in large quantities on those occasions when they could obtain it. The notorious speakeasies didn't exist before prohibition, when people could drink legally and leisurely. What we currently have is age-specific prohibition and young people are forced to create their own "speakeasies" in dorm rooms and other secret locations where they, too, must gulp their alcohol in the absence of moderating social control.

Dr. Hanson: You're saying that simply lowering the drinking age would solve the problem of drinking abuse among young people?

Dr. Engs: Unfortunately, it wouldn't solve the problem. However, it would be an important step in the right direction.

The experience of many societies and groups demonstrates that drinking problems are reduced when young people learn at home from their parents how to drink in a moderate and responsible manner. As parents we need to be good role models in what we say and do.

And lowering the drinking age would help send the important message that drinking is, in itself, not evidence of maturity…that responsible consumption for those who choose to drink is evidence of maturity.

We need to reinforce the norm of moderation by making it clear that the abuse of alcohol is completely unacceptable by anyone. This would help stress that it is not drinking that is the problem but rather drinking abusively that is the problem.

Dr. Hanson: These ideas may sound great, but would they really work?

Dr. Engs: These proposals are not based on speculation but on the proven example set by many societies and groups around the world that have long used alcohol extensively with very few problems.

On the other hand, our current prohibition directed against the consumption of alcohol by young people (who can marry, serve in the military, vote, enter into legal contracts, and shoulder adult responsibilities) is clearly not working. We need to abandon this failed and demeaning folly and replace it with a proven, realistic, and successful approach to reducing drinking problems.

---

*Reprinted from Alcohol Problems and Solutions (www.alcoholinformation.org) by permission of the authors.

Dr. Ruth Engs is Professor of Applied Health Sciences at Indiana University in Bloomington. Dr. Engs is the author of seven books, dozens of chapters and articles, and scores of scientific papers on alcohol. She is a leading, internationally recognized authority on drinking patterns and problems of college students; her opinions are sought by diverse groups and organizations.

Minimum Drinking Age

A misconception that many people have is that the minimum drinking age act prohibits underage "drinking." The act prohibits purchase and public possession, which are terms strictly defined and do not always mean consumption. For example, public possession does not apply to possession for an established religious purpose, when accompanied by a parent, spouse, or legal guardian age

21 or older. It also does not apply in the course of lawful employment by a licensed entity, such as a bar or restaurant. Each state is different in its specific prohibitions and how they are worded. In Georgia, for example, consumption implies possession, so any alcohol level on a breathalyzer, whether in a car or just in front of your own house or for that matter *in* your own house, can lead to a citation for minor in possession. In some places in that state the police may try to bust an underage adult in his or her own home who may be under the supervision of his or her parents.

Some states allow exceptions for minor consumption under supervision; some do not. Some states allow exceptions for consumption on private property with variations as to specific type of property in question. The exceptions may extend to all private locations or private residences only, or only to the home of a parent or guardian or legal-aged spouse. It is a good idea to carefully check the statutes for your individual state so that you thoroughly understand your rights before trying to defend them.

Other Countries

Almost all other countries have much more reasonable drinking age regulations. Some countries distinguish between drinks with fairly low alcohol content such as beer and wine, and stronger, spirit-based drinks. Beer is sold in vending machines in some places, such as Taiwan and Japan. Many countries have banned alcohol advertising aimed at the youth market.

Laws surrounding alcohol vary, but generally minors are not allowed inside of drinking establishments and are not allowed to purchase alcohol. In the United Kingdom, children may enter pubs in the company of an adult until 9 P.M., and those 14 and older may enter pubs unaccompanied if they order a meal. Some jurisdictions allow minors to drink in the privacy of their own home with their parents' permission, and others do not.

The rigor with which age restrictions are enforced varies considerably from place to place. In some countries, proof of age is usually requested of everybody, while in others it is usually requested only if the customer appears to be obviously underage. Establishments that require proof of age will request it either at the door or when alcohol is purchased; usually a driver's license, passport, or special proof-of-age card must be used for this purpose.

Minimum Drinking Age by Country

What follows is a table of drinking ages around the world and some further clarification of some terms. The United States is the only civilized country listed in the 21 column, and yet we have the most problems when it comes to young people and alcohol abuse. Why is that? Is it because it has now become the "forbidden fruit "of the transition to adulthood? Perhaps it's because the 21-year age limit is unrealistic and counterproductive to our society as a whole. Instead of setting proper examples at home and including our young adults in constructive alcohol education programs, we've acquiesced to the control-of-availability agenda and ignored the success that other countries have had with their policies. Sex education is taught at school and American families discuss safe sex from an early age. Why not responsible consumption?

Note that exact laws vary from country to country, and often between states or provinces. Laws on consumption of alcoholic beverages vary even more widely. In some countries all alcoholic beverages are illegal, often because of religious law.

COUNTRY	DRINKING AGE	PURCHASE AGE	NOTES
Albania	None		
Antigua	16		
Argentina	18		
Armenia	None		
Aruba	18		
Australia	18		
Austria	16 (beer and wine), 18 (spirits)		Some cities allow the purchase of spirits at 16
Azerbaijan	15	18	
Bahamas	18		
Barbados	18		
Belarus	18		

(continued)

COUNTRY	DRINKING AGE	PURCHASE AGE	NOTES
Belgium	None in private with a guardian	16 (beer and wine), 18 (spirits)	
Belize	18		
Bermuda	18		
Bolivia	17		
Brazil	18		
Bulgaria	18		
Cambodia	None		
Cameroon	18		
Canada	18–19 depending on the province		Legal drinking age on the province legislation falls under provincial jurisdiction.
China	None	18	
Colombia	18		
Costa Rica	18		
Curacao	18		
Czech Republic	18		
Denmark	None	16 (stores), 18 (in bars and restaurants)	
Dominican Republic	18		
Ecuador	18		

COUNTRY	DRINKING AGE	PURCHASE AGE	NOTES
Egypt	21		
Estonia	21		
Finland	None (technically: see notes)	18–20 depending on location and alcohol concentration	Finland does not have a minimum drinking age, but has a minimum possession age
Fiji	18		
France	16		
Germany	16(beer and wine) 18 (spirits)		
Georgia	None	16	
Greece	No age limit (stores), 18 (in bars and restaurants)		
Guam	18		Ballot initiatives pending to change to 21
Hong Kong (PRC)	None	18	
Hungary	None	18	Possession or consumption of alcohol by minors is not an offence but supplying them with alcohol is.
Iceland	20		
India	18–25 (varies by state)		
Ireland	18		
Israel	18		
Italy	16 (in bars and restaurants)		
Jamaica	18		

COUNTRY	DRINKING AGE	PURCHASE AGE	NOTES
Japan	20		Alcohol can be bought in some vending machines.
Kenya	18		
South Korea	From January 1st of the year the person becomes 18		
Latvia	None	18	
Lebanon	18	18	
Lithuania	None	18	
Luxembourg	17,18(see notes)	18	Minimum drinking age is 17 when accompanied by an adult
Macedonia	18		
Malaysia	18–21		The sale of alcohol to Muslims is illegal, as is consumption of alcohol by Muslims.
Mexico	18		
Moldova	No minimum age (beer), 18 (wine and spirits)		
Netherlands	None	16–18 (depending on alcohol concentration)	
New Zealand	18	18	
Nigeria	None		
Norway	18–20 (depending on alcohol concentration)		
Peru	18		

COUNTRY	DRINKING AGE	PURCHASE AGE	NOTES
Philippines	18	18	
Poland	None	18	
Portugal	18	18	
Puerto Rico	18		
Romania	18		
Russia	18		
Serbia and Montenegro	16		
Slovak Republic	None	18	
Slovenia	None	18	
Singapore	18	18	
South Africa	18		
Spain	18		
Sweden	18 in public	18–20 (depending on alcohol concentration and location)	
Switzerland	None	14–16 (beer and wine), 18 (spirits)	Age limit on beer and wine varies between cantons
Taiwan	18	18	
Thailand	None	17	
Trinidad & Tobago	18		

COUNTRY	DRINKING AGE	PURCHASE AGE	NOTES
Turkey	18		
Uganda	18		
Ukraine	18		
United Kingdom	5 in private (and with parental consent), 16 or 18 in public (see right)	18 generally but 16 in certain circumstances (see right)	Persons aged 16 and over can be served beer and cider (and wine in Scotland) if ordered with a meal in a restaurant or in a pub with an area specifically set aside for meals. Otherwise the minimum drinking age is 18.
United States	21	21	Some states do not specifically ban underage consumption. Some states have family member and/ or location exceptions to their underage consumption and possession laws.
Uruguay	18		
Venezuela	18		
Zimbabwe	18		

The common denominator worldwide is the prohibition of drinking and driving. Like the drinking age, the blood alcohol levels for legal intoxication vary from country to country and state to state. They are generally from 0.08 to 0.10 percent, which means 0.8 to 1 part alcohol per thousand parts blood, which is referred to as the blood alcohol concentration. I really wouldn't split hairs on this one; if you plan on drinking, also plan on not driving.

How much alcohol must be consumed to reach those levels? The following table provides an approximate guideline.

MALE BLOOD ALCOHOL CONCENTRATION GUIDE

Number of Drinks Per Hour	BODYWEIGHT IN POUNDS								
	110	120	140	160	180	200	220	240	
	PERCENT OF ALCOHOL IN BLOODSTREAM								
1	0.04	0.03	0.02	0.02	0.02	0.02	0.02	0.02	Driving
2	0.08	0.06	0.05	0.05	0.04	0.04	0.03	0.03	Skills
3	0.11	0.09	0.08	0.07	0.06	0.06	0.05	0.05	Impaired
4	0.15	0.12	0.11	0.09	0.08	0.08	0.07	0.06	
5	0.19	0.16	0.13	0.12	0.11	0.09	0.09	0.08	
6	0.23	0.19	0.16	0.14	0.13	0.11	0.1	0.09	
7	0.26	0.22	0.19	0.16	0.15	0.13	0.12	0.11	Legally
8	0.3	0.25	0.21	0.19	0.17	0.15	0.14	0.13	Intoxicate
9	0.34	0.28	0.24	0.21	0.19	0.17	0.15	0.14	d in all
10		0.31	0.27	0.23	0.21	0.19	0.17	0.16	States

2

FEMALE BLOOD ALCOHOL CONCENTRATION GUIDE

Number of Drinks Per Hour	BODYWEIGHT IN POUNDS								
	100	120	140	160	180	200	220	240	
	PERCENT OF ALCOHOL IN BLOODSTREAM								
1	0.05	0.04	0.03	0.03	0.03	0.02	0.02	0.02	Driving
2	0.09	0.08	0.07	0.06	0.05	0.05	0.04	0.04	Skills
3	0.14	0.11	0.1	0.09	0.08	0.07	0.06	0.06	Impaired
4	0.18	0.15	0.13	0.11	0.1	0.09	0.08	0.08	
5	0.23	0.19	0.16	0.14	0.13	0.11	0.1	0.09	
6	0.27	0.23	0.19	0.17	0.15	0.14	0.12	0.11	
7	0.32	0.27	0.23	0.2	0.18	0.16	0.14	0.13	Legally
8	0.36	0.3	0.26	0.23	0.2	0.18	0.17	0.15	Intoxicate
9	0.41	0.34	0.29	0.26	0.23	0.2	0.19	0.17	d in all
10	0.45	0.38	0.32	0.28	0.25	0.23	0.21		States

Questions

1. Is the minimum legal drinking age of 21 a federally mandated law?

2. What nation has the highest imposed drinking age?

3. What nation has the most problems with underage consumption?

CHAPTER THREE

Size Does Matter

We've learned a little history, a bit about what alcohol chemically is, and how it affects your body. We've also discussed the law, now it's time to learn how to responsibly enjoy a few drinks. (It bears repeating here: Never ever drink and drive. Period. If you follow this one rule, you'll avoid the most serious threat of ruining your life and possibly the life of another.) With alcohol as with life, moderation is the key. Although moderation is the key, respect is the issue. Respect for yourself and others will influence your actions and encourage moderation. Respect for yourself will convince you not to damage your health by over-drinking. Respect for yourself and others will encourage you to enjoy alcohol in social settings without embarrassing yourself. We've all seen a drunk; some of us have had the displeasure of an unwanted encounter with a drunk. Some of us have even *been* that drunk. Respect for yourself and others will enable you to enjoy the positive effects of alcohol without dealing with the problems that overindulgence can induce.

No matter what the situation, learn to stay in control. Don't allow that anticipated celebration to turn into a disaster because you "just wanted to let loose." Don't think that having completed that test you studied for all week or successfully closing a business deal gives you the right to "get wasted." The moment you decide to drink is the moment you accept the responsibility that goes with it. With alcohol, you must always be cognizant of where you are with it. The responsible, healthy method of alcohol consumption requires that you set limits on your consumption and keep track of the amount you consume —always.

Even though drinking alcohol is called "drinking," don't drink it to quench your thirst. Before consuming alcohol you should always make sure you are well hydrated. Drink plenty of water before your first drink; this will enable you to avoid gulping your first few drinks because of thirst.

Responsible consumption is a two-step process: (1) You must first assign the correct potency or strength to each drink you consume, and (2) you must keep a running count of how many *drink equivalences* you have had over a specific period of time. Three drinks over the span of two hours is not the same as three drinks in one hour.

Use the Drink Equivalence Formula

one beer = one glass of wine = one shot of liquor
(12 ounces)   (5 ounces)   (1.5 ounces of
                                            80-proof liquor)

It is amazing how many people think that one drink is whatever they have poured in whatever size glass or mug they have in their hand. Three shots of liquor and a little bit of mix is not one drink! Four beers in an over-sized mug is not one drink!

You must keep track of how much you consume. It is important to count each *drink equivalence* (DE). One beer is one drink and one glass of wine is one drink; one mixed drink may be more. You must be cognizant of how many shots (1.5 ounces), are used to make your drink of choice. Don't assume the margarita you ordered is one DE; it may be much more. A DE is simply 0.6 ounces of pure alcohol, which is the equivalent of one 12-ounce beer, one glass of wine, or one shot of liquor. It's amazing how, even those with experience, have fallen prey to losing count of their drinks. The result of losing count is often a combination of inebriation and hangover—or worse. The key to understanding your limit is to keep track of how much you've consumed using the drink equivalence as the measure. The accuracy of the level of drink equiva-lences (DEs) you assign to each drink you consume is necessary for this system to work. You must assign the correct weight or strength to each drink so you can keep track of the volume of pure alcohol you have consumed. Counting drinks is of no use if you underestimate their strength.

Assigning DE values is easy if you are making your own drinks and measuring the amount of liquor with a shot glass. Skipping the shot glass and just pouring be-cause you think you have an eye for what a shot looks like disrupts the system. It's also easy to assign values if you're drinking standard domestic beer or wine. Assigning DEs becomes more difficult when you're drinking at restaurants and bars. In these situations you can't be sure whether or not the bartender is under- or over-pouring. This can sometimes be controlled by insisting that the bartender measure the liquor, but many places are just too busy to do that.

Generally, the mixed drinks you order at a bar contain one shot or less of liquor. This is a generalization that does not apply if the bartender is a personal friend of yours. Usually it is safe to assign a DE of one to a run-of-the-mill mixed drink like a vodka tonic or a Seven and Seven because it is unlikely that the establishment wants to give you more than you paid for. Ordering doubles is also pretty straightforward, since you just double the DE. Assigning the correct potency, however, can get tricky if you order more complicated drinks like a martini or a Manhattan, which are usually worth two DEs.

In all of your approximations of the DE, it is always better to overestimate than underestimate. If you're not sure whether the drink is a one or a two, always assign a value of two, or at least a one and one-half; you'll be much happier the next day if you do.

The other point to remember is that not all beers are created equal. A beer labeled a malt liquor is stronger than an average beer. Belgian ales are also notoriously potent. Read the labels of these beers and find the percentage of alcohol by volume to determine the DE to assign to them. If the label indicates proof, divide that number by two to determine the percentage strength. Once the strength by percentage has been determined, it's an easy multiplication exercise to get to the actual amount of pure alcohol in the particular beer. Remember, we're assigning a DE of one to a pure alcohol content of 0.6 ounces, so in a 12-ounce beer that is observed to be 7 percent alcohol by volume, the equation would be:

12 ounces x .07 = .84 ounces of pure alcohol

The DE would then be .84 divided by .6, which is 1.4. The correct assignment of DE strength to this beer would, therefore, be about a 1.4, since a DE of one is .6 ounces of pure alcohol. Using this same logic, we can say that any 12-ounce beer with a strength of 5 percent alcohol by volume or less can be safely assigned a DE of one. If doing this math is too much like work, I'm including a table that does the work for you.

BEER	3%	4%	5%	6%	7%
16 OZ	.8 DE	1 DE	1.3 DE	1.6 DE	1.9 DE
12 OZ	.6 DE	.8 DE	1 DE	1.2 DE	1.4 DE

It Doesn't Matter What You Drink

It doesn't matter what you drink, or if you mix; alcohol is alcohol. What matters is the quantity you consume and the rate of consumption. There is no truth in the misconception that drinking different forms of alcohol is what makes you drunk or sick. If you drink six beers, do a few shots, and wash it all down with a bottle of cheap wine, don't blame the mix when you're praying to the porcelain god; blame yourself.

Keeping Track of Quantity

This part of the process sounds simple, but it really takes the most effort. It's easy to lose track of what you've consumed during the course of an evening with all the distractions that occur. You may be busy in conversation, listening to music, or watching a ball game. You may be at a crowded party or bar (assuming you're old enough), where the drinks are flowing and you're having a good time. Whatever the environment, you'll be much happier the next morning if you keep count. Distractions are no excuse. If you're going to drink, you must always be aware of how many drinks you have consumed.

Let's look at a possible scenario:

Your fraternity is (or was, if you are a more mature reader) having a keg party before the football game. You show up and stake your claim as the official bartender. Dispensing beer in front of the keg has huge advantages; it's not only a great place to meet women, it also ensures that you'll never have to wait to get your next beer. You pour a few and talk to friends, all the while filling your own cup at will. Some pledges come by with a few shots and of course you do a few; life is good, you're having a great time.

Everything goes well for a couple of hours, but then you find it strange that you can't speak very well anymore. When you take a break from your designated post you find yourself a little unsteady on your feet. You think you're fine and that no one will notice, but everyone does. When you speak to the next beautiful lady—who gets more beautiful with each drink—your words really don't sound like English anymore. On your way to the restroom you finish your beer and do another shot. How many is that now? It doesn't matter, you feel fine. You get to the restroom—and the next thing you know, you find yourself waking up in that restroom, and someone is pounding on the door and yelling for you to unlock it. When you get up and leave, you're not aware that several of your frat brothers are laughing *at* you. You do notice it is dark outside, and the house is almost empty. Where did the day go? Who won the football game? Why do you feel so bad? What happened?

What happened is you failed to follow the first rule of responsible consumption: Count each drink equivalence. You were having a great time hovering around the keg, but you lost track and you didn't count each drink. Hell, you didn't count any drinks. This is a perfect example of what a novice, uninformed drinker does—loses track and loses face all at the same time.

Count Your Drinks

There are several good techniques for keeping track of your drinks, and they vary depending on your situation and what you're drinking. From the keeping-track-of-your-drinks perspective, there are two major rules:

1. Always finish each cup or glass completely before filling your cup again. Finish each cup completely before topping off because you can't keep an accurate count if you're constantly filling a partially drained cup. This

holds true no matter what it is you are drinking. Be especially cognizant of this rule at keg parties. An over-zealous host can really wreak havoc with your count.

2. Pick a strategy to physically keep a running tab of how many drinks you have consumed. There are a variety of ways to do this, some of which are outlined in the following sections. Trying to mentally keep track of what you've drunk becomes very inaccurate as the night wears on. These miscounts tend to always favor the lower amount; it's funny how it works that way.

Beer

If you are at a keg party and drinking beer, you can use the same cup the entire time and make a mark for each beer on the cup with a pen. If you don't have a pen, you can use a fresh cup for every new beer and keep the stack in your hand. If you're drinking out of a soft material, such as Styrofoam, you can even make a bite mark on the cup or scratch the side with your fingernail. If you are drinking from bottles or cans, save the bottle caps or the pop tops. If you're doing beer bongs it won't matter; you'll be too drunk to count.

Mixed Drinks

Counting mixed drinks at a party is really no different from counting beer provided you are drinking out of paper or plastic cups. But if drinks are being served in a glass, you need a different technique. A good approach is to put a fresh straw or a stirrer in each drink, saving the previous one. If you wake up in a stranger's backyard with 18 straws in your pocket, you'll know why. You can even carry a marker and draw hash marks on the back of your hand if you have no other means of keeping count. The point is to keep track. Count each drink equivalence, and always use a shot glass when mixing drinks.

Wine

A bottle of wine generally contains about five glasses of a 5-ounce pour. The problem with wine is that it is often enjoyed with dinner, and during dinner it is very common for anyone and everyone at the table to constantly try to fill everyone else's glass. It is a social, courteous practice, but it makes it very difficult to accurately count how many glasses you've had. The trick here is to hold on to your glass, or at least keep it out of easy reach of the most conscientious filler. The advantage with wine is that it is usually enjoyed with food, so the drinking-on-an-empty-stomach aspect is avoided.

Shots

A shot can be consumed in just a few seconds; we already know the body can metabolize one DE an hour, so if you're going to drink responsibly, that one shot is all you get for an hour. Not much fun. Shots are dangerous for the simple reason that they are potent and are quickly consumed—and generally consumed after people have already had too much to drink. Since the effects of alcohol lag, if you're not careful you can easily consume several shots before you feel their effects, and then they'll hit you in the head like a ton of bricks. Doing shots in this manner often leads to severe drunkenness, blackout, or worse.

Shots are probably the most common reason for the intermittent memory syndrome, where memories of the night before are hazy or incomplete. Doing shots in this manner is also what leads to the infrequent but devastating occurrences of deaths due to alcohol poisoning. Our bodies just cannot handle high concentrations of alcohol so quickly. Avoid shots. They don't taste good, are hazardous to your health, and can drastically affect your self-control.

In all of these situations, and no matter what you are drinking, the bottom line is to count every DE, without fail, each and every time you enjoy a cocktail. *If you do this one thing—if you count every drink, every time—you'll avoid most of the problems associated with drinking.*

Understanding what a drink is and how to accurately rate a drink's potency using the concept of the drink equivalence, along with the acknowledgment that you should always be aware of your running count, will enable you to enjoy alcohol for what it is: a pleasant and healthy adjunct to an enjoyable life.

There are a few other good practices when it comes to drinking responsibly. Always note the time of your first drink in order to accurately assess your rate of consumption. Simply look at your watch and mentally note what time it is; this will help you avoid drinking too quickly and exceeding the one-drink-per-hour standard. Another great tenet is the guideline of "eight hours bottle to throttle," used in the aviation community. This is a standard protocol that is actually included in the Federal Aviation Regulations. It means that under no circumstances can a commercial airline pilot, or any pilot for that matter, have any alcohol at all within eight hours of flight duty. None.

This does not mean, however, that a pilot can get roaring drunk, just as long as he stops more than eight hours prior to duty. Sometimes eight hours is not nearly enough to recover from a session of irresponsible consumption, but at least it sets a minimum guideline responsible consumers can use. I think the same guideline can be used by anyone who wants to have a productive day following a night that included enjoying a few drinks. Eight hours bottle to throttle can become eight hours bottle to Business 101, or eight hours bottle to Chem 103. It can be eight hours bottle to negotiating a big deal or eight hours prior to getting to work. Remember this protocol: It just makes sense and can keep you feeling excellent each and every morning.

Questions

1. What are the two steps to responsible consumption?
2. What is the definition of the drink equivalence?
3. Are all beers created equal?
4. What are some good strategies for keeping track?
5. Is it important to note the time that you had your first drink?
6. What do we mean by eight hours bottle to throttle?
7. Why is doing shots a bad idea?

CHAPTER 4

Enough Is Enough

You've heard the old adage that everyone should understand his or her own limitations; this is especially true with alcohol.

Once you've developed a tracking system either using the suggested techniques of the last chapter or other techniques that work for you, discover your own individual limit. Keep in mind, however, that this limit should not be misconstrued as a badge of honor. There is no accomplishment in being able to drink more than anyone else. Being able to drink large quantities of alcohol without being visibly affected is not a talent or a skill; it does not indicate mental toughness or control. It simply indicates your body, under the present conditions, has a certain tolerance to alcohol. This tolerance is dependent on physiology and not on self-control. Your body size, the volume of blood in your body, the levels of ADH in your blood, and so forth are the factors affecting your tolerance. The things you can control that affect your limits are the speed at which you drink and whether or not you have food in your stomach when you are consuming alcohol.

Please keep in mind that your limit and the amount you normally consume are two entirely different things. You must determine your limit to enable you to stay in control, but you should not make it a habit to drink to your limit every time you have a few drinks. Alcohol in moderation is healthy but in excess can be toxic. Some research has suggested upper limits for moderate consumption as two to three drinks in a day for men and one to two for women. Other research indicates that there is no harm in consuming up to five drinks in a day for men, and up to three for women, but at these higher levels the benefits of alcohol are diminished. In the article "The Beneficial Side of Moderate Alcohol Use" (Turner 1981), Turner finds that, in general, chronic ill effects are restricted to heavy drinking of 5.7 drinks a day or more. More research is needed, but most of the studies show that the lower levels of moderate consumption are healthier, especially for the heart, than abstinence (Ford 2003). Keep in mind that there is a real danger in swift over-consumption as in the case of drinking several shots in succession. Every year there are lives lost due to alcohol poisoning from drinking too much too fast. Don't do it.

Although limits are an individual parameter, common sense comes into play. Drinking a 12-pack at a sitting is not a level I'd call a limit, I'd call it a mistake. Drinking a half bottle of bourbon is also not a limit or moderation; it is drinking to excess and should not be considered responsible consumption. With drinking, more is not better; moderation is better, control is better.

The only way to determine your own limit is through experimentation. Use your friends' observations to let you know if you've gotten noticeably inebriated, even if you haven't realized it yourself. How many drunks realize they're drunk? If you get to a point that you feel you shouldn't drink anymore, stop, note the amount that you've consumed and use that for future reference. If you drink to the point of feeling good and remaining in control, but you feel terrible in the morning, you've had at least one too many drinks. You should endeavor to never have the amount you drink today affect your productivity tomorrow. Your limit should be less than the amount that induces a hangover.

While determining your limit, keep in mind that although the quantity of your consumption is very important, the rate of your consumption is just as important. Make sure you note your rate of consumption in this experimentation phase. Try to limit yourself to one drink per hour. If you do that, you will probably avoid intoxication since, as mentioned before, the liver can handle about one drink per hour.

Another important aspect of any drinking strategy is the realization that drinking on an empty stomach has different consequences than drinking on a full stomach. Alcohol will affect you much more quickly with nothing to impede its progress through your stomach, into your small intestine, and then rapidly into your bloodstream. Food will slow down this rate of alcohol absorption.

The results of drinking on an empty stomach are that you'll feel the effects of the alcohol more quickly. Drinking on a stomach that is not empty will slow the rate of the alcohol's effects and might induce you to drink more, but it may enable you to have more control. The problem with drinking on an empty stomach is if you don't make sure you drink slowly, the pleasant relaxation you're expecting may be replaced by almost immediate intoxication. The problem with drinking on a full stomach is you may be tempted to drink more—and more quickly—since the rate of effect is less rapid. In fact, your limits will be completely different in these situations. You can consider yourself to have two limits: one with food and one without. Make sure you know exactly what to expect from yourself in both of these situations.

Be careful, though. A novice drinker who chooses to drink on an empty stomach may lose self-control and ignore his or her limits completely. This is a common reason people end up losing control. If you drink too quickly on an empty stomach you'll be affected almost immediately, and your self-control will become compromised. Drinking on an empty stomach is something that should be avoided until you have determined and understand your own limits in this situation. Always have food on hand when enjoying a few drinks. If you feel yourself getting too buzzed, stop drinking and eat; it will slow the effects of the alcohol still in your stomach—although, this should not be a situation you find yourself in since you will have determined your own limitations after having read this book, and you'll be prepared for any situation.

Let's look at another scenario:

You just completed the last of three tests for the week, which took an extensive amount of preparation. You studied hard and you're ready for a break. You had breakfast several hours ago and you're a little bit hungry but it's already 1:30 and you still want to work out and be able to make happy hour at 4:00. You decide to skip lunch and get the exercise in. You're psyched about getting those tests behind you, and you're so full of energy that you not only run several miles, but you also hit the weights for an hour.

Back at the dorm you take a beer into the shower from your well-concealed stash. It tastes exceptionally good today. The shower feels exhilarating, but you've got to hustle if you're going to make happy hour. You finish another beer while getting dressed and make a mental note to get some more beer for the stash. On your way out you realize you're not that hungry anymore.

You arrive at your favorite place for happy hour. It's your favorite place because the beers are only a quarter. You're having a great time talking, laughing, playing foosball, drinking beer of course, and munching on a few buffalo wings, but you're more thirsty than hungry and you really don't eat much.

After happy hour ends at 7 P.M., you head over to a friend's party—and free drinks. You eat a handful of nachos and pay for a full-priced beer before walking over to the party. It's only a few blocks away.

How many beers was that? You know you're supposed to keep track, but you forgot with all the fun you're having. Let's see, two at the dorm, three or was that four at the club? It doesn't matter because you feel just fine. The party is rocking and you know most of the people there. Some of your friends have a bottle of tequila and they offer you a shot, which, of course, you accept.

You wake up in your room—thankfully, since you don't know how you got there— feeling terrible. The last thing you remember is getting to the party. You feel bad, but worse than that, now you've got to call your friends to try to reconstruct what you did last night.

What happened? Drinking on an empty stomach is what happened. You were affected very quickly because there was very little food in your stomach to mitigate the effects of the alcohol you consumed. This situation often leads to a lack of control since it happens to you unexpectedly; you don't normally get that drunk on that amount of alcohol, so you're not ready for it.

Once again, accept the fact that you have two different intake limits: one limit for empty/almost empty stomach consumption and one limit with food in your stomach. Everyone metabolizes food at different rates, and different foods are easier to absorb than others, but if you've eaten within the past couple of hours, you probably still have some undigested food in your stomach.

Let's expand on the full stomach situation, which has its own set of problems. If you're really full you'll be tempted to overindulge, and go past your limit, since it will take alcohol longer to affect you. As previously stated, the presence of food will induce the pylorus to close to aid in digestion. Also, the alcohol will be absorbed into the food, further slowing the rate at which it is taken up into the bloodstream. People tend to over-drink in this situation because they're not experiencing the usual affects of a certain amount of alcohol. You might think: *These drinks must be watered down, I just don't feel anything yet.* Be very careful in this situation because when the stomach finally releases its contents into the small intestine, it's releasing all of that additional alcohol you've consumed trying to make up for the lack of the effect the same quantity of alcohol usually has. More alcohol may actually get into your system since the action of the alcohol dehydrogenase in your stomach will be somewhat impaired by the food that is present (Byerlein 1999). At this point you can get intoxicated very rapidly, being taken by surprise by the rapid change. If you're full, I recommend that you take it easy on the alcohol and allow your system time to digest the food. Also, drinking too much on a full stomach can make you sick to your stomach since the combination of alcohol, food, and acid sometimes just does not mix.

My recommendation is that if you choose to drink on an empty stomach, enjoy that first drink—but have food available to snack on to delay the effects of the subsequent drink. I also don't recommend drinking immediately after a big meal. Other than an after-dinner cordial, my drinking is usually terminated after a large dinner.

This book is about responsible consumption and with that responsibility comes the requirement for planning; planning when and under what situations you want to have a few drinks. Drinking on an empty stomach with no food available is bad headwork; continuing to drink on a full stomach is not a good idea either.

A good question right now would be what actually should be the limit? What behavioral outcome should you use to determine this limit? What physiological outcome? At this juncture I will tell you what not to use; do not *ever* drink to the point of blackout. Blackout is alcohol-induced amnesia, a dangerous situation. If you wake up not remembering what you did the night before, you've gone much farther than your limit. Your determination of your personal limit should be simple: never allow yourself to lose control, always be able to remember the night before, and don't wake up with a hangover. If you follow the guidelines set in this book, these three goals should be easy to reach.

The mistake many people make is they think the more they drink, the better they'll feel. The reality is the more they drink, the drunker they will be. This distinction between a pleasing buzz and getting drunk should be your goal. Remember, you should never feel remorse or shame after a night of drinking; if you do, you've gone too far. The buzz from alcohol lags, that is, *its effect is not immediate.* The buzz you feel is probably not from that drink in your hand, but from the one you consumed before. The one you're consuming now will become apparent later. This is why it's important to drink slowly, to determine your limit, and to not rely on how you may be feeling at the moment. Even though you feel fine, that drink in your hand may be the one that makes you act silly or the one that makes you feel slow in the morning.

The Effects Are Temporary

The pleasant effects from alcohol are temporary; accept this fact. Most uninformed drinkers assume that by continuing to drink, even after they've reached their limit, they'll continue to enjoy the pleasant effects alcohol can impart. The reality is they're about to become intimately familiar with the unpleasant effects a hangover can impart.

The buzz is the buzz. It won't get better. You can't make yourself feel better or enhance the effects by drinking more; you can only try to maintain the euphoric feeling for a period of time. At this stage, drink slowly and do not exceed your limit. At your limit, don't drink anymore. To delay reaching your limit, you can alternate between alcohol-containing drinks and soft drinks or water. This technique helps you avert the hassle of having drinks forced on you by an overzealous host or friend. Avoid that infamous nightcap. Having one last drink before turning in for the night is a waste of good liquor and may be the *one too many* that makes you feel terrible in the morning.

The Biphasic Effect
How Alcohol Affects Us: The Biphasic Curve
by David J. Hanson, Ph.D.

Most people think that if a few drinks make them feel good, then a lot of drinks will make them feel even better. But that's not true. Although a few drinks will make them feel better, more will make them feel worse. It's called the biphasic (or two part) effect.

Here's what happens. People tend to feel better as their blood alcohol concentration (BAC) rises to about .05 (.055 to be exact).

That's the first phase or part. If people drink more and their BAC rises above .055, the negative effects of drinking increase and hangovers become worse. That's the second phase. So it's clearly smart to stop during the first phase and not progress into the second phase.

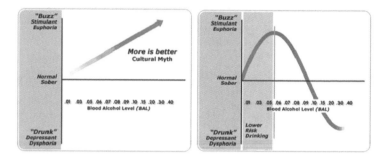

*Reprinted from Alcohol Problems and Solutions (www.alcoholinformation.org) by permission of the author.

These results were also substantiated in *The Better Way to Drink* (Volger and Bartz 1982):

In summary, since a BA above 55 (BAC above .55) loses its positive quality for most drinkers, and a rising BA feels much better than a falling BA, we can conclude that the most satisfying and successful way to drink is to start completely sober, drink for 30–45 minutes, and back down. That's the ideal way.

Remember, the amount of food in your stomach will affect the rate at which alcohol is absorbed into the bloodstream. Your emotional state or fatigue can also impact the effect that alcohol has on your system on that particular day. This means that your limits can change depending on the environment and your physical condition. You must be in touch with your situation; some days it would be prudent to decrease your personal limit. Again, please understand that I'm not suggesting you drink to your limit every time you enjoy a drink. The reality is you should drink to your limit infrequently. It's important to determine and understand your limit, but don't make drinking to your limit a habit.

We know the limit I keep mentioning is the point that you achieve the mellow feeling that moderate alcohol consumption can impart while still avoiding drunkenness. One way of ascertaining this limit is behavior, another is the hangover. As mentioned before, if you wake up hungover, you've exceeded your individual limit. Make it a point never to wake up hungover.

Having said this, I must mention that a lucky 25 percent of the population is not affected by the hangover. The disadvantage these people have is they have no causal physical effect of over-drinking. Their body does not let them know they've overdone it. This can be either a blessing or a curse, depending on how you look at it. People who pay no price in the morning for overindulgence may have a harder time controlling their consumption. They're not apt to "swear to God" they'll never drink again. They feel fine, but their bodies suffer the same inner harm as the rest of us. Alcohol is healthy in moderation but all of the benefits disappear and the harmful effects begin when taken in excess. These "lucky" people may actually be prone to develop bad drinking habits. If you happen to be in this category, be aware of your good fortune and don't abuse it.

Procedure for Responsible Consumption

1. Plan the situation. Make sure you have a nondrinking driver.
2. Prepare your body. Make sure you eat first or there is food available. Drink plenty of water.
3. Note the time you have your first drink.
4. Mentally restate your limit.
5. Count every DE.
6. Drink slowly.
7. Respect your limit.
8. Don't make drinking to your limit the standard.
9. "Eight hours bottle to throttle."

Guidelines for Drinking

- Never drink and drive.
- Never get into a vehicle with someone who's been drinking.
- Determine your limit.
- Keep track of your drink equivalence (count your drinks).
- Drink slowly.
- Do not participate in drinking contests or games.
- Understand that your limit can change depending on your condition (empty stomach, weight change, fatigue, emotional state, etc.).
- Avoid drinking on an empty stomach; have food available.

An easy way to remember the basics is to use the acronym for tender loving care:

T: Note the *time*

L: Remember your *limits*

C: *Count* your drinks

Questions

1. Is drinking on an empty stomach any different from drinking on a full stomach?

2. What is the biphasic effect?

3. What does it mean when we say the effects of alcohol lag?

4. Do all people who drink too much suffer from hangovers?

CHAPTER 5

Fit for Duty

When alcohol is ingested, the body treats it as if it were a toxin. Even though when taken in moderation, alcohol is beneficial, the body, on a cellular level, tries to eliminate it. There is a phenomenon called the "French paradox," which indicates that although the French eat more fatty and rich foods than Americans, they suffer much less from heart problems, hence the paradox (Ford 2003). Another interesting fact is that the French also drink more, and more often, than Americans. Researchers believe that this heart health paradox is associated with this more prevalent alcohol consumption. Research also suggests that moderate drinkers are more heart healthy than nondrinkers.

All this research is based on moderate rates of consumption that are usually defined to be no more than four drinks a day for a man and two for a woman. When alcohol is consumed in excess, we all know it can be damaging to the human body. That is why anything but responsible consumption is a huge mistake.

Keeping your body supplied with the necessary nutrients and staying physically fit through exercise is important not only for alcohol elimination but also for everyday life. If you ever skip a workout because you feel a little slow after a night of drinking, you haven't followed the policies set forth in this book; you haven't stayed below your limit. You should feel no different the day after having a few drinks than you do the day after having consumed no alcohol. If you count your DEs and stick to the plan, you won't suffer any ill effects.

Studies have shown that even those of us who eat a well-balanced diet do not get enough nutrients from the food we consume (Packer 1999). Our food lacks the basic vitamins and antioxidants we need to stay healthy. The National Cancer Institute recommends that we consume between seven and nine servings of antioxidant-rich fruits and vegetables a day. Seven to nine a day! How many of us do that? To make up for this nutritional deficit, additional supplementation is mandatory. Even the American Medical Association, which has traditionally scoffed at supplementation, has turned the corner. In a dramatic reversal of clinical opinion published in the June 2002 issue of the *Journal of the American Medical Association* and based on a Harvard Medical School study, the medical profession now recognizes the value of vitamin supplementation:

Suboptimal intake of some vitamins…is a risk factor for chronic diseases. Low levels of the antioxidant vitamins may increase risk for several chronic diseases. Most people do not consume an optimal amount of all vitamins by diet alone. It appears prudent for all adults to take vitamin supplements.

They get even more specific: "We recommend that all adults take a multivitamin daily" (Fletcher and Fairfield 2000). This is a complete turnaround from the AMA's previous philosophy that taking vitamins was a waste of both time and money. The fact is, most of us cook away a large portion of the antioxidants and vitamins in our foods, and those of us who make it a point to eat raw foods don't eat enough of them to get the full benefit supplementation provides. There have actually been hundreds of studies that support the need for vitamin supplementation, with an emphasis on antioxidants.

Those of us who choose to drink alcohol should especially pay attention to this research. When alcohol is ingested, the body treats it as if it were a toxin. Even though moderate alcohol consumption is beneficial, the body, on a cellular level, tries to eliminate it. The assimilation and elimination of alcohol uses up some of these nutrients at a higher rate, so those of us who drink should definitely consider daily vitamin supplementation.

Instead of going into the specific vitamins and minerals needed and for what reasons, and in order to avoid the need for people to come up with their own form of vitamin cocktail, I suggest taking a good absorbable multivitamin. Based on my own extensive research, I've decided on a system with which I'm really pleased. It consists of packets of capsules taken twice a day. The packets are very convenient and contain capsules that are very absorbable. One packet in the morning and one with dinner provide a very comprehensive supply of vitamins, minerals, and antioxidants. The point is to do some research and find a multivitamin that fits your own needs. These vitamins will also help your body recover more quickly if you should make the occasional mistake of overindulgence. For more information about supplements, please visit my website at www.ThinkingWhen Drinking.com or call 678-852-9659.

Preparation also includes deciding on where and when you're going to drink. Drinking is obviously not appropriate in all venues or all situations. There will be days you just don't feel like drinking, even if you're at a party or a bar. In these situations, have the good sense not to drink just because everyone else is drinking. Stay in tune with what your body is telling you.

Questions

1. What is the "French paradox"?

2. Do studies indicate that vitamin supplementation is necessary?

3. How many servings of fruits and vegetables should we try to consume daily?

CHAPTER SIX

Does My Head Look as Big as It Feels?

Although the hangover may seem to be a trivial or humorous matter (to those not suffering from it), it has significant economic ramifications. Studies have indicated that the effects of immoderate alcohol use accounted for more than $100 billion annually in the United States alone (Wiese et al. 2000). The misconception is that alcoholism is the culprit. Costs associated with alcoholism are definitely a factor, but the greater costs in the workplace are those incurred due to the decreased productivity of affected employees as a result of the common hangover. These costs include hangover-related absenteeism and poor job performance because of these hangover symptoms. A British study found that immoderate alcohol use accounted for 2 billion pounds ($3.3 billion U.S.) in lost wages each year, most of which resulted from work missed because of hangover (Crofton 1987). Alcohol costs in other countries have yielded similar results: Canada, $7.5 billion each year, $1.4 billion of which is lost because of decreased occupational productivity caused by hangover-like symptoms; Australia, \$3.8 billion; and New Zealand, \$331 million (Wiese et al. 2000).

This book is about responsible consumption, not about the type of overindulgence that leads to a hangover. Although I've warned you about limits and the avoidance of over-drinking, some of you will, at least once, ignore my suggestions and suffer the aftereffects of over-indulgence. My advice at this stage is to remember how badly you feel, so you never allow the situation that precipitated this feeling to occur again. Remember that dry, cottony, parched desert feel to your mouth. Remember that throbbing, exploding, pulsating headache. Remember that gnawing uneasiness. Hangovers are not funny, and they definitely are not healthy. They indicate that you did not exercise self-control the night before, and now your body is suffering the chemical and physical effects of mild alcohol withdrawal, which include:

- **Dehydration (dry mouth):** Alcohol is a diuretic; it causes the body to increase urinary output by inhibiting the release of antidiuretic hormone from the pituitary gland. Reduced levels of this hormone also prevent the kidneys from reabsorbing water, which in turn increases urine production (Swift and Davidson 1998). Four drinks can cause the elimination of up to a quart of water over a several hour period (Montastruc 1986 cited by Swift and Davidson 1998). Sweating, vomiting, and diarrhea also commonly occur during a hangover and contribute to overall dehydration and electrolyte imbalance. Symptoms of thirst, weakness, dizziness, and lightheadedness are common to both hangover and dehydration.

- **Fatigue and sleep disruption:** Although taking a drink or two before bedtime has been known to enhance the onset of sleep, overindulgence leads to fatigue caused by alcohol's disruptive effects on sleep. The sedative effects of alcohol make falling asleep easy; staying asleep is the difficult part. Alcohol interferes with the body's normal sleep patterns, changing the length of REM (rapid eye movement) sleep and the time spent in slow wave sleep. The body enters into a condition called rebound excitation, where, in response to or actually in its effort to counteract the sedative effects of alcohol, the body overreacts and actually enters a heightened state where sleep is more difficult. Also, since the body is forced to work harder to metabolize and eliminate alcohol, an increase in the normal pulse rate is observed, which makes sustained sleep difficult (Swift and Davidson 1998).

- **Headache:** Probably the most common manifestation described during a hangover is headache. Although common, the exact causes of the headaches have not been confirmed. Alcohol overindulgence results in vasodilatation, which can induce headaches by lowering the blood pressure. Dehydration also lowers the pressure in the cranial blood vessels, which compounds this problem (Braun 1996). Alcohol also has effects on several hormones and neurotransmitters that are implicated as contributors to headache.

- **Anxiety:** Sometimes described as the most uncomfortable of the hangover symptoms, anxiety encompasses many things: nervousness, restlessness, uneasiness, rapid pulse—an overall feeling that something is not quite right. Alcohol is a powerful drug and metabolizing it has an effect on many different systems in the body. Overindulgence disrupts those systems when the rate of consumption exceeds the body's ability to break it down. Hormones, neurotransmitters, enzymes, and many other chemicals that are powerful in their own regard are affected by alcohol and may play a role in the cause of anxiety. Evidence suggests that hangover-induced anxiety is a condition or state of central nervous system excitation. Following heavy or chronic alcohol exposure, the body decreases the number of gamma-aminobutyric acide (GABA) receptors, which are the body's primary means of inhibiting nerve cell activity. At the same time, the body increases the number of glutamate receptors, which are the body's primary means of exciting nerve cell activity to offset alcohol's sedative effects. When the alcohol is removed, the sympathetic nervous system remains in an unbalanced, heightened state of rebound excitation, which contributes to the feelings of anxiety as well as other symptoms, including sleep disruption and rapid pulse (Swift and Davidson 1998).

- **Nausea and vomiting:** Alcohol irritates the stomach and intestines and can cause inflammation of the stomach lining, which is called gastritis. Alcohol also induces the stomach to increase the production of gastric acid. These factors can result in the queasy stomach common to hangovers.

Imagine having all of these symptoms simultaneously; sounds like the start of a great day. And remember, the more you drink, the worse your hangover.

In the chapter on the properties of alcohol, I described the way alcohol is metabolized, and I mentioned that acetaldehyde is a byproduct of the first step in the breakdown of alcohol. Acetaldehyde is a toxic substance that binds to proteins and other biologically important compounds. It causes rapid pulse, sweating, nausea, vomiting, and skin flushing, if allowed to be present in high concentrations. In most people, acetaldehyde dehydrogenase metabolizes acetaldehyde quickly and efficiently, but if the body cannot keep up with the sheer quantity of alcohol present, acetaldehyde accumulates, and so do its effects. Some researchers believe that acetaldehyde has a large part to play in the cause of the hangover. It is also postulated that the reason some people don't suffer as much from hangovers is because their bodies metabolize the acetaldehyde much more efficiently than those that do suffer (Swift and Davidson 1998).

Congeners are also blamed for causing hangovers. I stated previously that congeners are biologically active compounds produced as byproducts during the production of alcoholic beverages. These compounds contribute to the smell, taste, and color of the beverages they are in. Congeners may be produced along with ethanol during fermentation; in fact other alcohols such as methanol are congeners. The byproducts of methanol metabolism, formaldehyde and formic acid, are highly toxic. Congeners are also produced during the aging process, or as stated above, added to the beverage for color or taste. Research suggests that those beverages with fewer congeners induce fewer hangovers than do beverages containing a larger number of congeners. Those that are purer in ethanol tend to be clearer in color, so vodka and gin tend to induce fewer hangover symptoms than those darker in color, such as whiskey, cognac, or tequila. Red wine is also blamed for more severe hangovers than white wine. However, don't be under the misconception that it's okay to drink as much as you want of that handle of vodka just because it's clear. If taken in excess, any form of alcohol can produce a hangover.

The whole point of this chapter is to emphasize that you should be able to control your drinking so you rarely suffer the debilitating effects of a hangover. There are no cures; if you wake up hungover you have failed! You can try drinking a lot of water or sweating it off with exercise, but you're going to suffer nonetheless. Use this misery as a lesson and remember how bad you feel so that the next time you find yourself tempted to get wasted by chugging twenty beers, you won't do it.

Just as an added word of caution: if you do end up with a headache I recommend you do not take acetaminophen (Tylenol). Over-drinking stresses the liver enough without the possible added liver toxicity of acetaminophen.

Questions

1. What is a hangover?
2. Is there a cure for the common hangover?
3. How is a hangover prevented?

CHAPTER 7

The Danger Zone

Drinking at more than moderate levels over a period of time can be severely detrimental to your health. The whole point of this book is responsible consumption, not the kind of abuse that can lead to the following problems.

Alcoholism

Here is the definition of alcoholism given by the American Medical Association:

Alcoholism is an illness characterized by preoccupation with alcohol and loss of control over its consumption such as to lead usually to intoxication if drinking is begun; by chronicity; by progression; and by tendency toward relapse. It is typically associated with physical disability and impaired emotional, occupational, and/or social adjustments as a direct consequence of persistent and excessive use of alcohol (*Manual on Alcoholism* 1968 as cited by Ford 2003).

Explaining alcoholism can be a complicated process because of the disparity of opinions as to what it is. Is it an actual physical disease, or an addiction due to a lack of will power or self-control? Is it genetics or the environment of our upbringing; is it nature or nurture, or both? Most researchers believe it is a combination of these factors. What most people agree upon is that an alcoholic cannot control his or her drinking and alcoholism is not simple alcohol abuse.

Alcohol Abuse

Any consumption that is socially offensive or dangerous to self or others is called alcohol abuse (Ford 2003). I'd go further to say that alcohol abuse is really self-abuse because, as we should all realize now, any alcohol consumption that is immoderate is harmful. Alcohol abuse can be chronic or occasional and falls short of meeting the definition of alcoholism. People who abuse alcohol may be said to have a drinking problem but having a problem does not necessarily mean they are, or eventually will become, alcoholic. Although the usual progression to alcoholism does include a period of abuse, the key is to avoid any irresponsible consumption to avoid these pitfalls.

The Brain

There is a difference of opinion on whether or not alcohol destroys brain tissue. It is true that alcohol is a powerful solvent that can be used as a disinfectant and can indeed kill cells, but these lethal levels of concentration are never reached in the brain. Remember, legal intoxication occurs anywhere between .08 to .10 percent;

this is a dramatically lower level than the concentration of the solutions used for sterilization (Braun 1996).

The position that alcohol does not directly kill brain matter was supported by a study that carefully counted the neurons in matched samples of alcoholics and nonalcoholics (Jensen and Pakkenberg 1993). The study used people who had died from causes unrelated to alcohol abuse. The results from the two groups showed no significant differences in either the number or the density of neurons present. There are, however, some contradictory studies that show patients with a history of chronic alcohol abuse have smaller, lighter brains than those of people who do not drink heavily (Rosenbloom 1995).

The truth is that even if alcohol at the concentration found in the brain were toxic, we have so many billions of brain cells that we could afford to lose a few and still not lose our minds. According to a study by Dowling (1992 as cited by Braun 1996), we naturally lose about 7 percent of our brain's neurons during the course of our lives due to normal wear and tear. That percentage equates to about 200,000 neurons daily (Braun 1996).

Even though alcohol does not necessarily kill those brain cells that we have so many of, we know from observation that chronic abusers of alcohol show clear signs of diminished cognitive ability. Alcohol affects so many neural transmitters and receptors that it is very difficult to ascertain exactly how chronic abuse modifies the brain. It may be that some of those receptors and ion channels become worn-out from overuse, or that the specific proteins and chemicals used in the communication of the neural synapses are depleted.

According to Roberta J. Pentney, professor of anatomy and cell biology at the University of Buffalo who has studied chronic alcohol abuse and brain function for almost 20 years, alcohol does not kill brain cells. Rather, it damages dendrites, the branched ends of nerve cells that are involved in neural communication. This damage causes a reduction in message traffic between neurons in this part of the brain. According to Dr. Pentney, these findings may relate to tremors and lack of coordination often observed in alcoholics. The research did show that this damage was a "reversible phenomenon. The brain was repairing itself after alcohol damage" (Baker 2000). The recovery or repair of the previously damaged dendrites is not identical to the structure before damage, so the neurons may not function in the same way. "We now had a model that might apply to what is happening in recovering alcoholics. Most of their motor functioning returns to normal, but some does not" (Baker 2000). Whatever the reasons for change in the functioning of the brain, chronic abuse of alcohol is definitely associated with cognitive dysfunction.

The damage that alcohol can induce is particularly harmful in the developing fetus. A study by Dr. John W. Olney, M.D., the John P. Feighner Professor of Neuropsychopharmacology at Washington University School of Medicine, indicates that a single instance of overdrinking by a pregnant woman might be enough to damage the brain of her unborn child. "Our animal studies indicate that significant nerve cell death occurs in the infant mouse brain following exposure to blood alcohol levels equivalent to those a human fetus would be exposed to by maternal ingestion of two cocktails" (Dryden 2004).

Olney's research has suggested that exposure to alcohol can cause developing brain cells to undergo neuroapoptosis—brain cell suicide. Olney points out it is clear that large doses of alcohol can trigger such extensive death of nerve cells in the developing brain that it causes a permanent reduction in the size of the brain and long-term cognitive impairment. Olney believes that the same type of pathological process can explain the harmful effects of alcohol on the developing human brain, a condition known as fetal alcohol syndrome "It's the best explanation that has been developed so far for the well known, devastating effects of alcohol on the human fetal brain," Olney says (Dryden 2004).

Olney believes it is unlikely that a single glass of wine would cause substantial damage to an expectant mother's fetus, even if that single glass were taken regularly. "A single glass is not a problem, but if one glass leads to another and then another on the same day, that is a different matter because then blood alcohol levels remain above the toxic threshold for too long, and nerve cells commit mass suicide," said Olney. Olney believes the safest practice for pregnant women is to completely avoid alcoholic drinks (Dryden 2004).

The research has demonstrated that mouse—and presumably human—brains are sensitive to the toxic effects of alcohol during a developmental stage known as synaptogenesis. It is a time when brain cells are furiously forming most of their synaptic connections. This brain growth spurt in humans lasts from the sixth month of pregnancy to a child's third birthday. During this brain growth spurt a single prolonged contact with alcohol lasting for four hours or more is enough to kill vast numbers of brain cells. "There is a massive wave of cell suicide after the brain is exposed to ethanol," says Olney. "The cells die by the millions and millions" (Dryden 2004). Nerve cells are genetically programmed to commit suicide if they fail to make synaptic connections on time. Alcohol interferes with the brain's neurotransmitter systems and with the formation of those synaptic connections, automatically activating a signal within the neuron that directs it to commit suicide—not a good thing for that developing brain.

The Liver: Alcohol-Related Liver Disease

The liver, being the main organ for alcohol metabolism, is particularly susceptible to alcohol injury. The first sign of alcohol related liver damage is a condition known as fatty liver where fat accumulates within the liver cells. In the early stages, this condition is reversible through abstinence and leaves no permanent damage (Ford 2003). If drinking continues, some drinkers develop alcoholic hepatitis, or inflammation of the liver. Its symptoms include fever, jaundice (abnormal yellowing of the skin, eyeballs, and urine), abdominal pain, changes in liver cell structure, and death of liver tissue.

Alcoholic hepatitis can cause death if drinking continues. If drinking stops, this condition often is reversible. Alcoholic cirrhosis, a deadly disease, occurs when scar tissue develops, replacing the now dead tissue, and can also cause death if drinking continues. Although cirrhosis is not reversible, one's chances of survival improve considerably if the drinking stops. Although a liver transplant may be needed as a last resort, many people with cirrhosis who abstain from alcohol may never need liver transplantation. In addition, treatment for the complications of cirrhosis is available.

Heart Disease

Moderate drinking can have beneficial effects on the heart, especially among those at greatest risk for heart attacks, such as men over the age of 45 and women after menopause. The risk of coronary heart disease appears to be lessened by the consumption of one or more ounces of pure alcohol daily, but long-term heavy drinking increases the risk for high blood pressure, heart disease, and some kinds of stroke. More than 3 ounces a day ushers in the risk of other health problems that could negate any benefit to the heart (Ford 2003).

Cancer

Long-term heavy drinking increases the risk of developing certain forms of cancer, especially cancer of the esophagus, mouth, throat, and voice box. Women are at slightly increased risk of developing breast cancer if they drink two or more drinks per day. Drinking may also increase the risk for developing cancer of the colon and rectum (NIAAA "Alcohol—What You Don't Know Can Harm You").

Pancreatitis

The pancreas helps to regulate the body's blood sugar levels by producing insulin. The pancreas also has a role in digesting the food we eat. Long-term heavy drinking can lead to pancreatitis, or inflammation of the pancreas. This condition is associated with severe abdominal pain and weight loss and can be fatal.

CHAPTER 8

To Your Health

With all the bad press alcohol gets, some people find it hard to believe that alcohol actually provides health benefits. Most people are familiar with the benefits associated with the heart. Numerous studies have indicated that daily moderate alcohol consumption decreases the incidence of coronary artery disease, reduces the frequency of heart attacks, and decreases the amount of time spent in hospitals.

Earlier I mentioned a phenomenon called the French paradox, and on the surface, it truly is a puzzle. Statistically, it seems the French enjoy much healthier hearts than we Americans. The puzzle is that they also consume a diet that includes much higher levels of animal fats than we do. They also exercise less, smoke more, and are generally less health conscious. What gives?

Their intake of alcohol, especially wine, is about 10 times higher than ours. Many have postulated that their daily alcohol consumption is what gives them the edge. There are volumes of scientific data that support the role of moderate alcohol consumption with reduced rates of coronary artery disease.

One of the best books I have found on the subject of the benefits of alcohol is *The French Paradox and Drinking for Health* by Gene Ford (2003). The book is based on thorough research, is easy to read, and offers excellent insight into the stigma attached to alcohol. In it you'll find that:

- Statistically, moderate drinkers live longer and experience fewer hospitalizations.
- Moderate drinking enhances human appetite, particularly in the aged.
- Alcohol reduces stress.
- Half of the hospitals in America make drinks available to their patients.
- Moderate drinkers suffer fewer heart attacks.

We all know that a small dose of aspirin taken daily can have beneficial results for the heart. But did you know that about the same time the heart-healthy benefits of aspirin became known, so did the heart-healthy effects of alcohol? "Analyses showed that compared with non-drinkers, people who drank moderate amounts of alcohol every day—defined as two beers or wines or one mixed drink, had a 49 percent lower risk of heart attack" (Hennekens as cited by Ford 2003). Dr. Charles Hennekens of Harvard Medical School was also on the team that discovered the widely publicized benefits of a 47 percent reduction in heart attack risk among those who take an aspirin every other day. Both of these studies were funded by the American Heart Association (AHA), but only the findings on the aspirin study were widely publicized. When asked about their reticence to publicize the positive results of the alcohol study, the AHA explained that they thought it unwise to do so because of the danger this information might lead to over-drinking (Ford 2003). Although the results clearly indicated moderate drinkers suffer from less coronary artery disease, they didn't think the general public could handle the information.

"The studies that have been done show pretty clearly that the chances of suffering a cardiac death are dramatically reduced by drinking one or two glasses of wine a day or equivalent amounts of alcohol" (Whitten 1987).

The authors of a study of more than 51,000 male professionals conducted at Harvard University found that men who drank, on average, three to four days per week had a lower risk of heart disease than men who drank less than one day each week (Rimm as cited by Ford 2003).

What follows is a fantastic synopsis of the benefits of alcohol from Gene Ford's book *The Science of Healthy Drinking*, compiled by Dr. David J. Hanson.

Healthy Drinking
by David J. Hanson, Ph.D.

The Science of Healthy Drinking by Gene Ford carefully analyzes the medical research evidence about the effects of drinking on human health and disease.

Some of the book's findings are listed here alphabetically. The numbers in parentheses refer to chapters in *Healthy Drinking*.

Acute Hospitalization (19)

Acute hospitalization refers to unscheduled visits to hospitals or emergency rooms. Research has discovered that moderate alcohol consumption dramatically lowers the risk of acute hospitalization.

• Moderate drinkers have dramatically fewer acute hospital visits than abstainers or abusers

• Some studies find that moderate drinkers have half the hospitalizations of abstainers

• Moderate drinking is associated with substantially lower hospitalization costs to society

Aging and Alzheimer's Disease (10)

Some research suggests that light drinking may delay dementia, loss of cognition, and Alzheimer's disease. Medical research indicates that light or moderate drinking

• Protects against cerebral lesions

• May delay the onset of Alzheimer's disease for as long as three years

• Is associated with slightly better cognitive (thinking) skills

• Is associated with an 80 percent decrease in frequency of dementia

All-Age Cognition (11)

Good cognition or normal reasoning faculties are important throughout life. Research has found that

• One to four drinks a day favors cognitive functions

• Moderate alcohol consumption increase happiness, euphoria, and carefree feelings

• Moderate consumption reduces the risk of poor cognitive performance

Angina Pectoris (1)

Alcohol and other components in alcohol beverages reduce the pain of angina and reduce the risk of heart attack. Moderate drinking has clear benefits, including

- Reducing both angina pain and heart attacks
- The reduction of vascular disease by one-third
- Reducing total mortality
- Lowering dangerous LDL cholesterol levels
- Producing serenity

Atherosclerosis (2)

The ability of moderate drinking to lessen the incidence of clogged arteries has been well known for at least 50 years. Medical research has demonstrated other important facts.

- Atherosclerotic build-up begins in childhood
- Daily alcohol intake reduces plaque build-up throughout life
- Moderate alcohol consumption lowers the bad (LDL) cholesterol
- Alcohol beverages provide more antioxidants than do vitamins C, E, and beta-carotene
- All types of drinks (beer, wine, and distilled spirits) fight atherosclerosis

Blood Clots (3)

Drinking lowers the incidence of blood clots. Alcohol

- Inhibits platelet growth
- Increases the body's production of the enzyme t-PA, which helps regulate fibrinolysis, which reduces the formation of blood clots

Breast Cancer (9)

The relationship between alcohol consumption and breast cancer is unsettled and unsettling. Some studies find a weak relationship while others find none. Alcohol may be involved in about 3 percent of breast cancers. Women should evaluate all risk factors, including family history of breast cancer. It's important to consider the comparative risks for heart disease and breast cancer. About half of all women will die from heart disease; about 4 percent will die of breast cancer. Research suggests that

- Breast cancer risk increases with advancing age
- Light alcohol consumption is not associated with breast cancer
- No causal link between alcohol and breast cancer has been established
- Heart attack deaths exceed those from breast cancer many times over
- The overall effect of moderate drinking is likely beneficial

Cancer (8)

Cancer refers to a very complex series of diseases (the four major types being carcinomas, lymphomas, leukemias, and sarcomas) that share common biological processes. Research suggests that

- Contrary to common belief, alcohol appears unrelated to cancers of the lung, bladder, prostate, stomach, ovary, and endometrium
- Two to three drinks a day reduces overall risk of cancer

Common Cold (12)

Americans spend hundreds of millions of dollars each year fighting the symptoms of the common cold. Fortunately, research suggests that alcohol can reduce the risk of contracting a cold by up to 85 percent. More research needs to be conducted, but the results are most promising.

Coronary Heart Disease (5)

Ischemia refers to an impairment of blood flow to the body's organs or the obstruction of an artery. Ischemia of the heart is coronary heart disease (CHD). Alternative terms are IHD (ischemic heart disease), CAD (coronary artery disease), and CHD (coronary heart disease). Medical research has found that

- Moderate drinkers have less ischemic disease
- Higher per capita drinking nations have less ischemia
- Higher per capita drinking states in the United States have less ischemia

Diabetes Mellitus (13)

Diabetes is a major disease that can lead to blindness and many other serious problems, and excessive consumption of alcohol must be avoided. However, research indicates that moderate drinkers are at reduced risk of developing Type 2 (adult-onset) diabetes. Medical evidence indicates that

- Moderate alcohol use is associated with lower incidence of diabetes
- Moderate drinking among male diabetics lowers their future risk of poor circulation

Essential Tremors (26)

Perhaps 5 million Americans, usually over 60 years of age, suffer from a condition called essential tremor (ET). Essential tremor usually involves the shaking of a body part, limb, or even the vocal cords. Although not life-threatening, essential tremor can seriously affect lifestyle. Many ET victims obtain relief from the tremor by consuming an alcohol beverage.

Gallstones (16)

Benefits of moderate drinking on gallstones identified by research include the following.

- Moderate drinking greatly reduces the risk of developing gallstones
- Drinking alcohol is associated with lower incidence of gall bladder disease
- Female drinkers have a 30 percent lower risk of gallstones
- Frequent, not infrequent, drinking provides risk reduction for gallstones

Gastro-Intestinal Problems (17)

Research demonstrates that moderate alcohol consumption can help calm the stomach the same way Pepto-Bismol does.

- Alcohol promotes the flow of saliva for good digestion
- Alcohol induces better absorption of nutrients
- Some alcohol beverages have proven more effective than Pepto-Bismol

Heart Attacks (6)

The American Heart Association describes a heart attack:

The medical term for heart attack is myocardial infarction. A heart attack occurs when the blood supply to part of the heart muscle (the myocardium) is severely reduced or stopped. This occurs when one of the arteries that supply blood to the heart muscle is blocked. The blockage is usually from a build-up of plaque (deposits of fat-like substances) due to atherosclerosis. A heart attack is often caused by a blood clot forming in a coronary artery....Such an event is sometimes called coronary thrombosis or coronary occlusion (*The Science of Healthy Drinking*, p. 66).

Heart attacks are the major cause of death and reducing them is a major objective of public health. Research has repeatedly found that

• Long-time drinkers suffer fewer damaging heart attacks
• Drinking reduces the risk of heart attack even among the overweight or obese
• Moderate consumption of alcohol can lower the risk of heart attack by up to one-half

High Blood Pressure (Hypertension) (4)

A very high proportion of middle-aged adults and older people suffer hypertension. While regular light drinking reduces high blood pressure, it is essential that drinkers stay within moderate consumption levels. Research demonstrates that

• Regular light drinkers experience fewer pressure-induced strokes
• Light drinkers exhibit desirable blood pressure profiles
• Risk advisories are directed exclusively against heavy drinking

Mortality and Morbidity (22)

Morbidity refers to disease and mortality refers to death, both of which are undesirable. Research indicates that moderate drinkers tend to be healthier and to live longer than do abstainers or abusers of alcohol.

- Research demonstrates a reduction of premature death for moderate drinkers compared to abstainers ranging from 10 to 40 percent
- Abstinence and abuse of alcohol are risk factors for both morbidity and mortality

Osteoporosis (23)

Over 25,000,000 Americans suffer osteoporosis or erosion of bone density. Fortunately, research demonstrates that moderate alcohol consumption can be beneficial.

- By 75 years of age, one in three men will suffer osteoporosis.
- Higher bone density is found among people who consume 12 drinks per week
- Women who drink at least seven ounces of alcohol a week have higher bone densities and
- Post-menopausal women who drink have stronger bones

Strokes (7)

Strokes occur when an artery supplying blood to part of the brain ruptures or becomes blocked, leading to the death of brain cells. Stroke is the third leading cause of death and a leading cause of long-term disability in the U.S. Research has demonstrated that

- Rates of stroke differ among different racial and ethnic groups
- Light consumption of alcohol lowers the risk of ischemic stroke, by far the more common type
- Abstention from alcohol increases the risk of ischemic stroke

- A diet including fruit, vegetables, fiber, mono-unsaturated fats, and moderate alcohol consumption reduces the risk of ischemic stroke

Ulcers (27)

It's ironic that alcohol, which was once thought to be an irritant for stomach ulcers, turns out to provide protection against them. Medical research has made major discoveries about ulcers, their cause, and treatment.

- Nine out of 10 ulcers are caused by a bacterium, *H. pylori*
- Alcohol appears to exert a protective effect against *H. pylori*
- Moderate drinkers are less likely to suffer duodenal ulcers

*Reprinted from Alcohol Problems and Solutions (www.alcoholinformation.org) by permission of the author.

Please remember that all these beneficial effects of alcohol are associated with light to moderate consumption. Even daily light to moderate consumption has been found to do no harm. If the use of alcohol becomes excessive, however, all the benefits are lost, and it becomes very harmful, as we have already mentioned. Moderation is the key, and if it can't be followed then it would be more prudent not to drink.

The research varies about what the upper limits should be as they relate to health. The upper limits range from two to five drinks for men and one to three for women. These particular limits are the point at which the health benefits are lost and the ill affects of heavy drinking become more likely. Look at it this way: There is a quantity of alcohol that is beneficial, there is a range that is not beneficial but is not harmful, and finally, there is a point at which alcohol consumption becomes harmful. The bottom line is that alcohol can be a friend or a foe, depending on how much *you* decide to drink!

CHAPTER 9

Working for a Living

Social settings in the business world can be a lot more important than just having a good time. Entertaining important clients graciously can be the difference between closing a major deal or losing one. Rubbing elbows with the bosses at an office party can lead to that promotion you've been seeking. Hosting that international delegation at a golf outing may mean future big business. Presiding over a companywide business presentation at the annual meeting in Hawaii can be the stepping stone to executive row.

As all of these situations provide excellent opportunities, they can also be monumental disasters if you fail to present yourself in a professional manner. Just one drunken scene in front of the wrong people can be the end to a promising career. Even if your superiors start getting carried away with their partying, do not join in; always be the one who stays in control. Be the one that keeps things together.

All the procedures for moderate consumption apply even more so in social, professional settings. No matter how beautiful or relaxing the venue, remember you are constantly being evaluated. Remember the fundamental guidelines discussed in this book to enable you to stay in control. It is important to keep track of your DEs and remember your limits, but a few more techniques may be of some value:

- **At restaurants and bars, be the one who buys.** This gives you the direct control over the number of drinks you consume, because, as you're buying the next round, you can exclude yourself and no one will be the wiser. You simply hang on to the same drink or have the bartender give you a soda.

- **Skip rounds.** Very simply, nurse your drinks and skip a few rounds. If you've got a drink in your hand, chances are your host won't be too pushy when it comes to offering you another drink.

- **Be the designated driver.** This is a great way to both limit your consumption and be a great guy to have around. This allows your clients to look at you as the person they can count on.

Company Functions

Do not drink during the day. Don't participate in the poolside all-day happy hour activities. This will keep your mind clear for the evening festivities and almost guarantee that you'll remain impressively professional all day and night long. You don't want to be the one taking a dip with all your clothes on or telling the boss you think he's a jerk.

Here's a friend's story:

"George" is a top executive with a software company whose duty it is to host his company's annual meeting for executives and management. It is a high visibility function where it is important to make a good impression. Typically, wives are invited to these meetings.

George had meetings all day, so he couldn't join his wife, "Linda," at the pool. Linda had a great time with the other wives and started drinking at about 1:00 when she was heard to say, "Oh, what the hell, it's five o'clock somewhere." The problem was that Linda didn't eat, but she drank all afternoon. George made arrangements to meet his wife at about 6:00 for an early dinner, before his annual presentation to the company.

When Linda didn't show for their dinner date, George thought she was just running a little late and would be there soon. A half-hour later, George went looking for her. George found his wife sitting in the auditorium still wearing her swimsuit, although this presentation was a formal affair. George knew he was in trouble as soon as he laid eyes on Linda, who had that distinct drunken dazed look in her eyes. George knew he was in real trouble because on the few occasions he had seen Linda in this state, she was very ornery. Although she fought all the way back to the room, George was able to put her to bed without too many of his colleagues being the wiser.

George was a bit nerve-racked by the time he got to the podium, but he wasn't noticeably late. Unfortunately, Linda showed up in the auditorium, heckling her husband for locking her in her room. It was a scene from hell that people in George's company still bring up when they're feeling exceptionally sadistic.

Linda ignored the basic rules on consumption. She drank on an empty stomach, she didn't count her DEs, and she started drinking too early in the day.

The Office Party

Office parties can be career enhancing; they can also be the career kiss of death. The most common reason these functions can get people into trouble is because they often occur after work, which is several hours after lunch but before they've had dinner. People anticipate this time when they can let their hair down, and reach for a drink before eating any of the usual snacks that are available. They begin talking and forget about counting their drinks or eating—a very dangerous combination. People have been known to be a little too honest with the boss or worse yet, they try to drive home when they shouldn't be behind the wheel of a car.

As in every other drinking situation, stay in control and follow the drinking guidelines.

The Business Lunch

Do not drink at a business lunch, period. Although the two-martini lunch used to be a common occurrence years ago, it is not common any longer and should be avoided. Most businesses expect a full day's work and drinking is not conducive to productivity.

This all may seem like common sense, but sometimes a review is a good idea, no matter how experienced you are.

CONCLUSION

Learning to drink responsibly is a requirement for anyone who chooses to drink. Take it from someone with more than 30 years of drinking experience, which includes my time in college and the U.S. Navy, and the last 18 years as an airline pilot. People who haven't seen you in years will remember, and bring up, the embarrassing moments in your life when you didn't practice responsible consumption. They won't remember your name, but they will remember, with uncanny detail, those scenes you'd like to forget. At that moment, all the great things you've done will take a backseat to those vivid descriptions of you in a compromising situation. Don't give them the ammunition; practice responsible consumption, or just don't drink.

Embarrassment is one thing, but much more serious consequences can occur if you don't control your drinking. Every year thousands of people ruin marriages, lose jobs, and worst of all, kill themselves and others by allowing their drinking to get out of control. If you enjoy alcohol, understand that you may have to give it up forever if you can't control it. If you don't practice responsible consumption from the onset, you may develop the routines that lead to problem drinking and alcoholism. If you cannot control your drinking, stop. Some people, whether due to genetics or environment, or both, just should not drink. It's really not worth ruining your life; if you can't enjoy alcohol in a controlled manner, don't drink. Freedom and life is about options. You can keep your options open by practicing moderation, not just with alcohol, but with all things. Drinking is not for everyone; it's not a requirement, but from the moment you intend to participate in it, you assume a responsibility to yourself and the rest of society. Society deserves and expects that those who consume alcohol do it in a way that does not compromise the safety of others. Never getting behind the wheel of a car after drinking and learning how to drink in moderation fulfill most of those responsibilities of the individual consumer.

I also believe U.S. society bears some of the responsibility for providing those who choose to drink with the logical, practical education necessary to drink responsibly. Our ambivalence about alcohol must end. The fact is that alcohol is legal and available; as long as it remains so, education about its use should be available. Although the control-of-availability agenda is trying to decrease alcohol consumption through misinformation, they are wrong to think that providing education about alcohol endorses its use.

We should strive to develop a comprehensive system of alcohol education that sets guidelines for responsible use, as well as employ strategies, such as social norms marketing, to reduce alcohol abuse. Most young adults falsely assume that a much larger proportion of their peers abuse alcohol than actually do. Using social norms marketing, this disparity in perception, that not "everyone" abuses alcohol, is highly reported and publicized. This leaves individuals who are exposed to this information feeling empowered to reduce their abuse of alcohol.

As stated previously, we've been teaching our children sex education from a young age, not because we were encouraging sex, but because we were acknowledging that empowering them with knowledge was much better than the dangerous alternative of keeping the information from them. In this case ignorance is not bliss; it is downright dangerous. The misuse of alcohol through ignorance is at least as dangerous. Providing this responsible alcohol consumption education simply makes us all much safer, and helps our young men and women avoid ruining their lives unnecessarily. This handbook is a perfect start in that education process.

According to Dr. Elizabeth Whelan, president of the American Council on Science and Health (1995):

In parts of the Western world, moderate drinking by teenagers and even children under their parents' supervision is a given. Though the per capita consumption of alcohol in France, Spain and Portugal is higher than in the United States, the rate of alcoholism and alcohol abuse is lower. A glass of wine at dinner is normal practice. Kids learn to regard moderate drinking as an enjoyable family activity rather than as something they have to sneak away to do. Banning drinking by young people makes it a badge of adulthood—a tantalizing forbidden fruit.

Although statistics indicate that it is on the decline (Johnston et al. 2006), teenage binge drinking can and does lead to sorrow for some families. We've discussed how confusing it is that a country with the most restrictive drinking policies suffers the most from the consequences of those policies. The control-of-availability agenda proposed by the government, the defamation of all alcohol usage, and the raising of the minimum drinking age are likely to continue to have an adverse impact on drinking patterns. These ill-conceived and ineffective strategies are also likely to increase abusive behavior, particularly in the young. These conclusions are derived from a 40-year study as reported in *The Natural History of Alcoholism* (Vaillant 1983).

Whether or not you agree with my view on the drinking age, we are faced with the fact that even though 21 is the magic age for legal consumption in this country, that does not change the fact that most young adults will drink alcohol before they reach that age. We, as a society, should not keep young adults from alcohol with the threat of punishment; rather we should empower these young men and women with the education of responsible consumption, and in doing so, give them the tools to make sound, informed decisions.

If you take anything away from this book, remember this: **Learning to drink responsibly is a requirement for anyone who chooses to drink.** And remember to use tender loving care:

T: Note the *time*

L: Remember your *limits*

C: *Count* your drinks

GLOSSARY

Absinthe is a spirit drink made with aromatics including star anise, fennel seed, and crushed wormwood leaves. It is green in color but turns white when water is added.

Acetaldehyde is a byproduct in the breakdown of alcohol that is toxic and is thought to contribute to the hangover.

Ades are tall warm-weather drinks consisting of sweetened lemon or lime juice and distilled spirits, garnished with fruit. They may include plain or soda water.

Alcohol refers to ethyl alcohol or ethanol, the type found in alcohol beverages. It is also commonly used to refer to alcohol beverage in general. The word alcohol is from the Arabic "al kohl," meaning the essence (CH_3CH_2OH).

Alcohol dehydrogenase is an enzyme that initiates the breakdown of alcohol into acetaldehyde.

Alcohol-related auto accidents are defined by the U.S. National Highway Traffic Safety Administration to include any and all accidents in which any alcohol has been consumed, or is believed to have been consumed, by the driver, a passenger, or a pedestrian associated with the accident. Thus, if a person who has consumed alcohol and has stopped for a red light and is rear-ended by a completely sober but inattentive driver, the accident is listed as alcohol-related, although alcohol had nothing to do with causing the accident. Alcohol-related accidents are often mistakenly confused with alcohol-caused accidents.

Ale is a style of beer made with top-fermenting yeast. Ales are typically hearty, robust, and fruity. See also: *Beer.*

ALS is the acronym for administrative license suspension (sometimes known as administrative license revocation), which is the temporary and almost immediate removal of a person's license if the person refuses to take or pass a BAC test. Thus, ALS does not require a conviction to occur and appears to be an effective practice in reducing drunk driving.

Amaretto is a liqueur made from apricot pits with a slightly bitter almond flavor.

American Council on Alcohol Problems is a temperance organization that promotes the control-of-consumption (more accurately called reduction-of-consumption) approach to reducing alcohol problems. See also: *Anti-Saloon League.*

Anisette (ahn-i-*set*) is a fragrant liqueur with a licorice flavor made with anise seeds.

Anstie's limit is the amount of alcohol that Dr. Francis E. Anstie (1833–1874) proposed, on the basis of his research, could be consumed daily with no ill effects. It is 1.5 ounces of pure ethanol, equivalent to two and one-half standard drinks of beer, wine, or distilled spirits. Today, we know that moderate alcohol consumption is associated with better health and greater longevity than is either abstention or heavy drinking.

Anti-Saloon League was a major organization involved in bringing about national prohibition in the United States. It is now, combined with the American Temperance League, known as the American Council on Alcohol Problems and actively attempts to influence public policy. It promotes the control-of-consumption (more accurately called reduction-of-consumption) approach to reducing alcohol problems. See: *Control of consumption.*

Aperitif (ah-pair-ee-teef) is an alcohol beverage typically flavored with herbals such as fruits, seeds, flowers, or herbs.

Applejack is a sweet apple-flavored brandy. Aqua vitae or "water of life" is the original name given to distilled spirits, which were first made for medicinal and health purposes. Scientific medical research has now made clear that the moderate use of distilled spirits or any other alcohol beverage is associated with better health and greater longevity than is either abstinence or heavy drinking.

BAC is the acronym for blood alcohol concentration or the proportion of alcohol in a person's blood. For example, 80 milligrams of alcohol in 100 milliliters of blood can be expressed as .08, .08 percent, or 80 mg percent. Also referred to as blood alcohol level or BAL.

Bacchus (bock-us) is the mythological god who was said to have spread wine culture throughout Europe.

Barrel is a standard unit of volume. A U.S. barrel is 31.5 gallons; a British barrel is 43.2 gallons.

BATF is the acronym for the Bureau of Alcohol, Tobacco and Firearms, an agency of the U.S. government that regulated those products until 2002. Under the Homeland Security Act of that year, BATF's alcohol beverage tax and regulatory functions were transferred to the new Tax and Trade Bureau.

Beaujolais (bo-jo-lay) is a light, fruity red wine produced in the Beaujolais region of France.

Beer is a fermented beverage made from barley malt or other cereal grains. Lager beer is a light, dry beer. Ale is heavier and more bitter than lager. Bock beer, porter, and stout are progressively heavier, darker, richer, and sweeter.

Beer Institute is the trade organization for the malt beverage industry in the United States.

Belgian lace refers to the white pattern of foam from the head of beer that is left on a glass after the beverage has been consumed.

Binge drinking traditionally and clinically refers to drinking in which the binger is continuously intoxicated for a period of at least two days, during which time the binger drops out of usual life activities such as going to work, meeting family responsibilities, and so forth. In recent years some activists have used the term to refer to situations in which a man consumes as few as five drinks in a day or in which a woman consumes as few as four drinks in a day. Such a misuse of the term dramatically increases the number of individuals who are categorized as bingers and has been criticized as misleading and deceptive by numerous professional organizations.

Bitters is a type of aperitif or cordial with a bitter taste used primarily to flavor mixed drinks.

Blue laws, believed to be so-named because they were originally printed on blue paper in the 1600s, regulate both public and private conduct on the Sabbath. Historically, they have prohibited such things as shaving, dancing, singing, traveling, cooking, working, and engaging in commerce. Today blue laws commonly prohibit the purchase of alcohol beverages on Sundays or Sunday mornings in an effort to promote church attendance.

Bock is a very strong lager beer traditionally brewed to celebrate the approach of spring. Bocks are typically full-bodied, malty, and well-hopped. See also: *Beer.*

Bodega is a Spanish wine cellar. Also refers to a seller of alcohol beverages.

Bordeaux (bore-doe) is a large wine growing region in southwestern France. Includes the areas of Medoc (meh-doc), Pomerol (paw-meh-rawl), St. Emilion (sant eh-mee-lyon), and Sauternes (saw-tairn).

Bottled-in-bond whiskey is straight whiskey produced under U.S. government supervision for tax purposes.

Bottom fermentation occurs when *saccharomyces carlsbergensis* ("lager yeast") is used in fermentation. This strain of yeast settles to the bottom of a tank during fermentation.

Bourbon is a beverage that is distilled from a mash of at least 51 percent corn and aged in new charred oak barrels. It was first produced by Reverend Elijah Craig in Bourbon County, Kentucky.

Brand name means proprietary name. The term originated from the practice among American distillers of branding (or burning into the wood) their names and emblems on their kegs before shipment.

Brandy is a beverage distilled from wine or fermented fruit mash. The word is from the Dutch *brandewijn*, meaning burnt (or distilled) wine.

Breathalyzer is a device used to measure blood alcohol concentration by measuring the alcohol content of a person's exhaled breath.

Brief intervention is a technique used to help individuals either abstain or reduce their use of alcohol and can be very effective.

Brown ale is a British-style, top-fermented beer that is lightly hopped and flavored with roasted and caramel malt.

Brut (brute) refers to dry Champagne. It refers to brutally dry.

Burgundy is a wine district in France. It is generically used to refer to other wines that resemble those produced in Burgundy.

Cabernet Sauvignon (*cab*-air-nay *so*-vee-n´yohn) is the most important red grape variety in the world.

Calvados (*col*-va-dose) is apple brandy distilled from cider in the town of the same name in northern France where it is produced.

Canadian whiskey is blended of straight whiskeys (usually rye, corn, and barley) distilled only in Canada under government supervision.

Cassis (kah-*seece*) is a purple liqueur made from currants.

Center for Alcohol Studies is the pioneering center for alcohol research located at Rutgers University.

Century Council is an organization dedicated to reducing drunk driving and underage drinking.

Chablis (shah-blee) is a dry white wine made from Chardonnay grapes in the Chablis region of France. It is also used generically to refer to other wines that resemble the wine produced in Chablis.

Champagne is an effervescent wine made in the Champagne region of France, generally blended from several different years and from as many as 40 different wines. Occasionally a vintage is of such a superior quality that a vintage Champagne is produced. Sparkling wines from other areas of the world are sometimes generically labeled champagne, but increasingly producers elsewhere are now correctly and accurately labeling such wine "sparkling wine."

Chardonnay (*shar*-doh-nay) is a white grape variety that is widely planted around the world and can produce fine wine.

Chenin Blanc (sheh-nan blahn) is a versatile white grape variety widely grown in California and South Africa.

Cherry brandy is distilled from cherries and is often called by its German name, kirchwasser.

Chianti (k'*yahn*-tee) is a wine from the Tuscany region of Italy.

Cider refers to unfermented apple juice in the United States but to fermented apple juice in the rest of the world. In the United States, fermented apple juice is called hard cider.

Cognac (*cone*-yack) is brandy distilled from wine in the Cognac region of France. Thus, all cognac is brandy but not all brandy is cognac.

Cold duck is a mixture of red and white sparkling wine that has a high sugar content.

Congeners (*khan*-gen-ers) are biologically active compounds that are byproducts of the fermentation process that lend taste and color to the beverage. They are thought to be contributing factors associated with the common hangover.

Control of consumption refers to an approach to reducing alcohol problems that attempts to do so by reducing the consumption of alcohol. It is more accurately called the reduction-of-consumption approach. Its ultimate goal is to re-establish the prohibition of alcohol. Currently being promoted by many governments and temperance groups. Also called public health model, neo-prohibitionism, and the new temperance movement. See also: *Drinking pattern*.

Cooler is a beverage made with a base of beer, wine, or spirits combined with ingredients such as fruit or cocktail flavors.

Cordial is liqueur made in the United States. Corn whiskey is distilled from a mash of at least 80 percent corn.

Cream ale is a blend of top- and bottom-fermented beers. It is typically sweet and lightly hopped.

Curacao is a cordial flavored with sour orange peel.

Denatured alcohol is ethyl alcohol that is made undrinkable by the addition of nauseating or poisonous substances.

Density of alcohol outlets refers to the number of alcohol beverage retail sales locations per unit of population or area of land. Research suggests that increased density follows, rather than causes, demand for alcohol beverages.

Designated driver is a person who does not drink at an event and drives others home. The use of designated drivers is widespread and has likely resulted in saving thousands of lives.

Distilled spirits refers to ethanol that is produced by heating fermented products, such as wine or mash, and then condensing the resulting vapors. Sometimes referred to as liquor or hard liquor. The term hard liquor is misleading in that it implies that the product is more intoxicating or potent than beer or wine. In reality, a bottle or can of beer, a five-ounce glass of dinner wine, and a shot of distilled spirits (gin, vodka, etc.) each contains an equivalent amount of alcohol.

Draught beer is keg beer served on tap. Sometimes called draft beer, which is how it is pronounced.

Drink equivalence is a term used to quantify the potency of an alcoholic drink. It equates to .6 ounce of pure alcohol and is equal to one 12-ounce beer, one glass of wine, or one shot (1.5 ounces), of 80-proof liquor.

Drinking pattern refers to such factors as the typical or characteristic quantity, frequency, speed of consumption, location, reason for drinking, and other characteristics of drinking as distinct from simply the quantity of alcohol consumed. The same quantity of alcohol consumed in different patterns can have vastly different consequences. For example, consuming two drinks a day (14 drinks per week) is associated with better health and longevity than is abstinence or heavy drinking. However, consuming 14 drinks once a week is associated with negative outcomes. This important distinction, along with many more, is ignored by the control-of-consumption (more accurately called reduction-of-consumption) approach to reducing alcohol abuse, which incorrectly assumes that simply reducing average consumption reduces alcohol problems.

Drug Free Schools and Campuses Act is a federal law designed to eliminate alcohol and drugs from all schools and colleges throughout the U.S.

Dry refers to the absence of sugar or sweetness in a beverage. It also refers to political subdivisions or areas in which the sale of alcohol is prohibited or to individuals who advocate prohibition.

Dublin stout is a very bitter and dark style of beer.

DUI is the acronym for driving under the influence of alcohol or other substances.

DWI is the acronym for driving while intoxicated or driving while ability is impaired by alcohol or other substances. Impairment can also be caused by other factors, such as sleep deprivation.

Eggnog is a beverage made with milk, whole eggs, and nutmeg. Brandy is then added if an alcoholic beverage is desired.

Eiswein (*ice*-vine) is wine made from frozen grapes (German). Same as ice wine.

Extra dry, when referring to sparking wines, actually means sweet.

Fermentation is the process during which yeast converts sugar into alcohol and carbon dioxide.

Finish is the lingering aftertaste that results after an alcohol beverage is swallowed.

Fizzes are mixed drinks of distilled spirits, citrus juices, and sugar shaken with ice. "Fizz" (soda water) or other carbonated beverage is then added.

Fortified wine is wine to which alcohol has been added to increase the proof to a higher level than the maximum possible from fermentation

Gin is distilled spirits flavored with juniper berries. It may also include additional flavorings. Although gins may be aged, producers of those sold in the U.S. are prohibited from reporting that they have been aged or, if so, for how long they have been aged.

Graduated licensing is a multistage program to allow new drivers on-the-road driving experience under conditions of reduced risk. It typically involves a beginning stage during which driving is permitted under supervision followed by a stage of unsupervised driving under restricted conditions, such as during daylight hours and with a limited number of passengers.

Grappa is Italian brandy made from pomace, which refers to the seeds and skins that remain after wine making.

Grenadine is a nonalcoholic syrup made from a variety of fruits and is used to flavor alcoholic drinks.

Grog is rum diluted with water. It is also an early English name for Caribbean rum.

Hair of the dog is a colloquialism that refers to the theory that the effects of a hangover can be minimized by drinking a small portion of alcohol when suffering from a hangover.

Hangover is the unpleasant consequence of over-consuming alcohol. It is characterized by headache, fatigue, and often nausea. It can be prevented by not over-consuming alcohol.

Harm reduction refers to policies or programs that reduce the harm that can occur as a result of alcohol abuse. Harm reduction can involve teaching moderation, promoting the use of designated drivers, improving highway safety, reducing drunk driving, and so forth.

Highballs are made with almost any distilled spirit, ice, and any of a number of carbonated beverages.

Hogshead usually refers to a 60-gallon oak barrel.

Hops is the small cone-shaped flower of a vine (*humulus lupulus*). Some varieties contribute mainly bitterness to brews, while others contribute aromas. Hops were originally used to preserve beer.

ICAP is the acronym for the International Council on Alcohol Policies, which is a public interest organization that seeks to reduce the abuse of alcohol worldwide.

Ice wine is made from frozen grapes. Same as *eiswein* (German).

Ignition interlock is a device that requires a person to blow into a breathalyzer before starting the engine of an automobile on which the interlock is installed. If the breathalyzer detects no alcohol, the interlock will permit the engine to be started.

Imperial stout is a very strong, dark, fruity beer. See also: *Beer*.

India pale ale was originally an ale brewed in England for British troops stationed in India during the 1700s. It was brewed very strong to survive a voyage that could last as long as six months and was highly hopped to help preserve it.

Irish whisky is triple distilled, blended grain spirits from Ireland.

Jamaican rums are medium heavy-bodied rums produced in Jamaica.

Jigger is a container for measuring liquids when making mixed drinks.

Juleps are traditionally made from Kentucky bourbon and fresh mint leaves. However, they can be made with gin, rye, brandy, rum, or champagne.

Keg is a measure of volume. A keg of beer contains 1,984 ounces.

Kentucky whiskey is a blend of whiskeys distilled in Kentucky.

Kosher wines are those produced under the supervision of a rabbi so as to be ritually pure or clean. Although commonly sweet, they need not be so.

Lager is a beer style made with bottom fermented yeast and is generally smooth and crisp. See also: *Beer.*

Legal drinking age refers to the minimum age at which alcohol beverages may legally be consumed. It is distinct from legal purchase age, which is the minimum age at which alcohol beverages may legally be purchased.

Legal purchase age. See: *Legal drinking age.*

Legs are the streams of liquid that cling to the sides of a glass after the contents have been swirled. Commonly believed to be an indicator of quality, there is little evidence to support this belief. Also called *tears.*

Light beer is reduced-calorie beer created by removing dextrine, a tasteless carbohydrate. Although beer, wine, and spirits all contain calories, their consumption does not appear to increase weight.

Liqueur (li-*cure*) is a sugared and flavored distilled spirit.

Liquor historically referred to any alcohol beverage but today it generally refers only to distilled spirits.

Liter is a measure of volume equal to 33.8 ounces.

London dry gin is an unsweetened gin.

Maceration is the process of placing crushed fruit into distilled spirits for a period of time in order to impart the flavor of the fruit.

MADD is the acronym for Mothers Against Drunk Driving, an organization that strongly and actively opposes any driving after the consumption of any alcohol.

Magnum is a bottle holding 1.5 liters or the equivalent of two regular bottles.

Malt (or malted barley) is barley that has been moistened, allowed to germinate, then dried.

Malt beverages are brewed from grain that has been permitted to sprout and is then dried. Such grain is called malt and contains much more sugar than un-malted grain.

Malt liquor is not liquor or a distilled spirit of any kind. It is a beer with higher alcohol content and often sweeter taste than most other beers. See also: *Liquor.*

Maraschino cherries are tart cherries from Dalmatia, used to garnish drinks.

Mash is ground malt (germinated barley) mixed with water.

Mead is a beverage made by fermenting honey mixed with water.

Merlot (mair-*lo*) is a red grape variety that can produce fine wine. It is often blended with Cabernet Sauvignon.

Mescal is a distilled spirit made from the dumpling cactus plant in Mexico.

Methuselah is a large bottle holding six liters or the equivalent of eight regular bottles.

Minimum drinking age is sometimes called legal drinking age. See also: *Legal drinking age.*

Minimum purchase age is sometimes called legal purchase age. See also: *Legal drinking age.*

Mixed messages are identified by some as messages that do not convey a single viewpoint.

Moonshine is an illegally produced distilled spirit. It is profitable to produce this illegal and sometimes dangerous product because legal spirits are very heavily taxed.

Mountain dew is another name for moonshine. See also: *Moonshine.*

Mull is a sugared and spiced hot drink made from a base of beer, wine, or distilled spirits.

NCADD is the acronym for the National Council on Alcoholism and Drug Dependence.

Neat refers to serving an unmixed, noniced distilled spirit in a glass.

Nebuchadnezzar is a large bottle holding 15 liters, or the contents of 20 standard bottles.

Neutral spirit refers to ethyl alcohol of 190 proof or higher than has no taste of the grains or fruits from which it was made.

NIAAA is the acronym for the National Institute on Alcohol Abuse and Alcoholism, a U.S. agency that supports and conducts biomedical and behavioral research on the causes, prevention, consequences, and treatment of alcohol abuse and alcoholism. It promotes the control-of-consumption (more accurately called reduction-of-consumption) approach to reducing alcohol abuse problems. See also: *Control of consumption.*

Oktoberfest is a beer festival held annually in Münich for 16 days and nights in late September and early October. Originated to celebrate a royal wedding in 1810.

On the rocks refers to serving a beverage poured over ice cubes.

Ouzo (ooze-oh) is an anise-flavored brandy-based Greek liqueur.

Package store is another name in the United States for liquor store. Package stores sell "package goods" because of laws requiring that alcohol containers be concealed in public by being placed in paper bags or "packages."

Petite Sirah (puh-tee see-rah) is a red grape grown in California. Not to be confused with Syrah.

Port is a fortified dessert wine from Oporto, Portugal.

Porter is a very dark, top-fermented beer. See also: *Beer*.

Price elasticity refers to the extent to which changes in the price of a product influence demand for that product. Price increases have the least impact on individuals who are addicted to alcohol. Therefore, raising the cost of alcohol beverages has little impact on their consumption.

Prohibition refers to legally attempting to prevent the production and consumption of alcohol beverages. National prohibition has been tried in numerous countries around the world during the twentieth century but has always failed and always been repealed. It is the ultimate goal of the control-of-consumption (more accurately called reduction-of-consumption) approach to reducing alcohol abuse.

Proof refers to the alcohol content of a beverage. In the United States, proof represents twice the alcohol content as a percentage of volume. Thus, a 100-proof beverage is 50 percent alcohol by volume and a 150-proof beverage is 75 percent alcohol. In the Imperial system, proof (or 100 percent proof), equals 57.06 percent ethanol by volume, or 48.24 percent by weight. Absolute or pure ethanol is 75.25 over proof, or 175.25 proof.

Pub is short in the United Kingdom for public house for drinking, as contrasted to a private house or club.

Public Health Model is another name for the control-of-consumption (more accurately called reduction-of-consumption) approach. See also: *Control of consumption.*

Puff is a traditional afternoon drink made of equal parts of a spirit and milk, to which club soda is added and then served over ice.

Punch is a drink mixture prepared in large quantities and is typically made with citrus juices and two or more wines or distilled spirits. Carbonated beverages are often included. Hot punches often use milk, eggs, and cream as a base.

Reduction of consumption is a more accurate name for control of consumption. See also: *Control of consumption.*

Rehoboam is a large bottle holding 4.5 liters, or the equivalent of six regular bottles.

Rice wine. See: *Saké (saki).*

RID refers to Remove Intoxicated Drivers, which is the oldest anti-drunk-driving organization in the United States. RID also fights nonalcohol offenses that are associated with traffic accidents and fatalities, such as reckless driving or driving with bald tires.

Robert Wood Johnson Foundation promotes the control-of-consumption (more accurately called reduction-of-consumption) approach to reducing alcohol problems. See: *Control of consumption.*

Rock and rye is a liqueur originally made from rye whiskey and rock candy.

Root beer is a nonalcohol beverage that was developed by temperance activists in the hope that it would replace real beer in popularity.

Rosé wines (ro-zay) are red wines that have not been permitted to have long contact with the skins of the red grapes from which they are made.

Rum is a beverage distilled from fermented molasses.

Rye whiskey is distilled from a mash of at least 51 percent rye grain.

Saké (or saki) is a fermented drink made from rice that is very popular in Japan. Although commonly called rice wine, it is actually a beer.

Sambuca is an Italian licorice-flavored liqueur made from elderberries.

Sangarees are made with whiskey, gin, rum, or brandy with port wine floated on top. Alternatively, they are made with wine, ale, porter, or stout with nutmeg. Not to be confused with sangria. See also: *Sangria.*

Sangria is a tart punch made from red wine along with orange, lemon, and apricot juice plus sugar.

Schnapps (schnopps) is a spirit distilled from potatoes or grain. Called schnapps in Scandinavian countries and Germany; it is called vodka elsewhere.

Scotch whisky is a blend of whiskies generally aged up to 10 years (about four years on average). Its characteristic smoky flavor results from drying malted barley over peat fires.

Sherry is a fortified wine that has been subjected to controlled oxidation to produce a distinctive flavor.

Shiraz (shee-*raz*) is the Australian name for the Syrah grape.

Shooter is a mixed drink, served straight up in a small glass, to be swallowed in one gulp. Differs from neat because it is served with a mixer.

Single malt Scotch whisky is unblended Scotch whisky. They vary substantially in characteristic depending on the mash from which they are made but all exhibit the unique smoky flavor of any Scotch whisky.

Sling is a tall drink made with lemon juice, sugar, spirits, and club soda.

Sloe gin is not gin but a brandy-based cordial made from sloe berries (the fruit of blackthorn bushes).

Social norms marketing is a highly effective method of reducing alcohol abuse. It is based on the fact that most people falsely believe that a much larger proportion of their peers abuse alcohol than actually do so. When the actual incidence of alcohol abuse among those peers is widely reported and publicized, individuals feel empowered to reduce their abuse of alcohol. It has consistently proven to be very effective.

Sommelier (so-mel-yay) is French for wine waiter or server.

Sour mash whiskey is made from a mash containing about 25 percent residue from a previous mash, which provides additional character to the resulting whiskey.

Sours are made with lemon juice, ice, sugar, and a distilled spirit.

Sparkling wine is carbonated wine.

Speakeasy was an establishment in which people could consume illegal alcohol beverages during national prohibition in the United States (1920–1933). The name is derived from the fact that people often had to whisper a code word or name through a slot in a locked door to gain admittance.

Spumantes are effervescent wines from Italy; *spumante* means sparking in Italian.

Stout is a very dark, heavy, top-fermented beer. See also: *Beer.*

Sulfites are naturally occurring compounds that prevent microbial growth. They are found on grapes, onions, garlic, and many other growing plants.

Swizzles are made of lime juice, sugar, a distilled spirit, and bitters packed with shaved ice.

Syrah (see-rah) is a red grape variety. It is especially important in the Rhone Valley of France. Not to be confused with Petite Sirah.

Tannin is a naturally occurring astringic acid found in many alcohol beverages that imparts a slight dry "puckering" sensation in the mouth.

Teetotaler is a person who abstains from alcohol.

Temperance is a term that referred to moderation in the 1700s and early 1800s. However, the word was later used by prohibitionists to refer to abstinence. Thus, the temperance movement is now associated with the Woman's Christian Temperance Union (WCTU), the American Council on Alcohol Problems (formerly existing separately as the Anti-Saloon League and the American Temperance League), the federal Center for Substance Abuse Prevention (CSAP), the Center on Addiction and Substance Abuse (CASA), the Center for Science in the Public Interest (CSPI), the Marin Institute, and increasingly, Mothers Against Drunk Driving (MADD). Such groups are more often referred to as prohibitionist or neo-prohibitionist rather than temperance groups.

Tennessee whiskey is made in compliance with the regulations for making bourbon but is charcoal filtered immediately after distillation. See also: *Bourbon.*

Tequila is distilled from the Mescal Blue or Tequilana Weber agave plant in Mexico.

Thief is a tubular instrument for removing a sample from a cask or barrel.

TIPS is the acronym for Training for Intervention Procedures by Servers of Alcohol, which is a program to teach servers responsible alcohol service.

Toasting is drinking an alcohol beverage along with a statement wishing good health or other good fortune. It is said to have started in ancient Rome, when a piece of toasted bread was dropped into the beverage.

Toddies are made of sugar water, a distilled spirit, and either ice or hot water to which is added clove, nutmeg, cinnamon, or lemon peel.

Tonic is a tall drink made of ice, a spirit, and tonic water.

Triple sec is a cordial flavored with the bittersweet oils of orange peels.

Varietal wine refers to a wine that is made primarily from one variety of grape. In the United tates, at least 75 percent of the wine in the bottle must be made from one variety for the bottle to carry the name of that variety. Therefore, in order to be labeled Cabernet Sauvignon, at least 75 percent of the wine in the bottle must be made from Cabernet Sauvignon grapes.

Vehicle impoundment refers to the confiscation of an automobile by law enforcement officers. It can occur in those jurisdictions that permit such impoundment when a driver has been determined to have been driving while intoxicated or with ability impaired.

Veisalgia is the medical term for the common hangover

Vermouth is a wine that has been soaked with as many as 40 flavorful aromatic herbs.

Viniculture is the art and science of making wine. Also called enology (or oenology). Not to be confused with viticulture. See also: *Viticulture.*

Vinification is the process of making grape juice into wine.

Vintage technically means harvest. When a vintage year is indicated on a label, it signifies that all the grapes used to make the wine in the bottle were harvested in that year. Except in the case of French Champagnes, vintage is not a clear indicator of quality.

Viticulture is the cultivation of grapes. Not to be confused with viniculture. See also: *Viniculture*.

Vodka, or "dear little water" in Russian, is a beverage distilled from potatoes or grain (usually corn and wheat). Most American-made vodka is filtered through charcoal. Some vodka is sweetened and flavored.

WCTU is the acronym for the Woman's Christian Temperance Union, an organization that was pivotal in bringing about national prohibition in the United States. It is still a very active organization promoting the control-of-consumption (more accurately called reduction-of-consumption) approach to reducing alcohol abuse. See also: *Control of consumption*.

Wheat beer is produced from a mash that includes wheat. The resulting beer varies from light and fruity in the United States to a dark bock in Germany.

Whiskey is a spirit distilled from grain in the United States, Canada, or Ireland (note spelling and compare to "whisky").

Whiskey bead is the stringlike circle of bubbles formed by whiskey when poured into a glass or shaken in a jar. It is said that the higher the proof, the more uniform and long lasting the bubbles.

Whisky is a spirit distilled from grain in Scotland (note spelling and compare to whiskey).

White lightning is another name for moonshine, or illegally produced distilled spirits. It is profitable to produce because of the very high taxes on legally produced spirits.

White Riesling (*reece*-ling) is a white grape variety widely planted in cool regions of the world. Called Riesling in Germany, Johannesberg (yo-*hahn*-iss-bairg), and the United States.

Wine is fermented juice of grapes.

Wine Institute is the trade association of California wineries.

Wort (vort) is the sweet liquid mash extract that is food for yeast that produces alcohol and carbon dioxide.

Zinfandel is a red grape variety widely planted in California although it is not, contrary to common belief, native to that state.

Zombie is a cocktail containing pineapple juice, orange juice, lime juice, apricot brandy, rum, and powdered sugar.

Zymase is an enzyme associated with the fermentation process.

BIBLIOGRAPHY

American Medical Association, *Manual on Alcoholism*, 1968.

Baker, Lois. "Brain Drain." *UB Research Quarterly,* 10; 1 (2000).

Beyerlein, Frederick M. *Drink as Much as You Want and Live Longer.* Port Townsend, Washington: Loompanics Unlimited, 1999.

Braun, Stephen. *Buzz.* New York: Oxford University Press, 1996.

Crofton, J. "Extent and Costs of Alcohol Problems in Employment: A Review of British Data." *Alcohol,* 22: 321–5, 1987.

Dowling, J. E., *Neurons and Networks.* Cambridge: Harvard University Press, 1992.

Dryden, Jim. "The Developing Mind: Small Amounts of Alcohol May Cause Damage." *Record,* 28: 22, 20 Feb 2004. http://record.wustl.edu/news/page/normal/2970.htm.

Engs, Ruth C. "Past Influences, Current Issues, Future Research Directions." *Learning About Drinking,* eds. Eleni Houghton and Ann Roche, 193–208. Philadelphia: Brunner-Rutledge, 2001.

Fletcher, Robert H., and Kathleen M. Fairfield. "Vitamins for Chronic Disease Prevention in Adults." *JAMA,* 287:23 (2002): 3127–29.

Ford, Gene. *The Science of Healthy Drinking.* South San Francisco: The Wine Appreciation Guild, 2002.

———. *The French Paradox and Drinking for Health.* South San Francisco: The Wine Appreciation Guild, 2003.

Forney, P. D., M. A. Forney, and W. K. Ripley, "Alcohol and Adolescents. Knowledge, Attitudes, and Behaviour." *Journal of Adolescent Healthcare,* 9 May 1988: 194–202.

Hanson, David J. "Formal Education." *Learning About Drinking,* eds. Eleni Houghton and Ann Roche, 193–208. Philadelphia: Brunner-Rutledge, 2001.

———. *Alcohol Education: What We Must Do.* Westport, Connecticut: Praeger, 1996.

———. "Binge Drinking." Alcohol Problems and Solutions website. http://www2.potsdam.edu/hansondj/BingeDrinking.html.

———. "Healthy Drinking." Alcohol Problems and Solutions website. http://www2.potsdam.edu/hansondj/HealthIssues/1055517115.html.

———. "It's Better to Teach Safe Use of Alcohol." *Alcohol Problems and Solutions.* http://www2.potsdam.edu/hansondj/YouthIssues/1044361545.html.

———. "The Drinking Age Should Be Lowered." Interview with Dr. Ruth C. Engs. Alcohol Problems and Solutions website. http://www2.potsdam.edu/hansondj/YouthIssues/1053520190.html.

Heath, Dwight D. "Teach Safe Drinking to Your College-Bound Teen." *The Addiction Letter,* 11:8, unpaginated special insert (1995).

Hennekens, C. American Heart Association, News Release, Abstract # 1990, Dallas, Nov. 19, 1987.

Holladay, April. "Does Alcohol Kill Brain Cells?" *Wonderquest.com,* 28 March 2001. Interview with Dr. Roberta Pentney. http//www.wonderquest.com/ BrainCells.htm.

Johnston, L. D., P. M. O'Malley, J. G. Bachman, and J. E. Schulengerg. "Monitoring the Future: National Results on Adolescent Drug Use. Overview of Key Findings." NIH Publication No. 06-5882. National Institute on Drug Abuse (2006).

Jensen, G. B., and B. Pakkenberg. "Do Alcoholics Drink Their Neurons Away?" *Lancett*, 342: 1993, 1201–04.

National Institute on Alcohol Abuse and Alcoholism, *Ninth special report to the U.S. Congress on alcohol and health.* Rockville, Maryland: NIAAA, 1997.

National Institute on Alcohol Abuse and Alcoholism, *Subcommittee of the National Advisory Council on Alcohol Abuse and Alcoholism—Review of Extramural Research Portfolio for Prevention*, October 21–22, 1998, Washington, D.C.

National Institute on Alcohol Abuse and Alcoholism, *Alcohol—What You Don't Know Can Harm You* (2004).

Perdue, W. Lewis, and Wells Shoemaker. *The French Paradox and Beyond.* Sonoma, California: Renaissance Publishing, 1992. http://www.french-paradox.net.

Roche, Ann M. "Drinking Behavior: A Multifaceted and Multiphasic Phenomenon." *Learning About Drinking*, eds. Eleni Houghton and Ann Roche, 1–33. Philadelphia: Brunner-Rutledge, 2001.

Rosenbloom, M. J., A. Pfefferbaum, and E. V. Sullivan. "Alterations Associated With Alcoholism." *Alcohol Health Res World*, 19(4) : 266–272, 1995.

Schippers, G., et al. "Acquiring the Competence to Drink Responsibly. " *Learning About Drinking*, eds. Eleni Houghton and Ann Roche, 35–56. Philadelphia: Brunner-Rutledge, 2001.

Swift, Robert, and Dena Davidson. "Alcohol Hangover—Mechanisms and Mediators." *Alcohol Health & Research World* 22(1), 1998.

Turner, T. B., V. L. Bennett, and H. Hernandez. "The Beneficial Side Effects of Moderate Alcohol Use." *The Johns Hopkins Medical Journal*, 148(2): 53, 1981.

Vaillant, George E. *The Natural History of Alcoholism.* Cambridge: Harvard University Press, 1983.

Volger, R., and W. Bartz, *The Better Way to Drink.* New York: Simon & Schuster, 1982.

Whelan, Elizabeth. "Perils of Prohibition: Why We Should Lower the Drinking Age to 18." *Newsweek*, May 25, 1995.

Wiese, Jeffrey G., Michael G. Shlipak, and Warren S. Browner. "The Alcohol Hangover." *Annals of Internal Medicine*, 132(11): 897–902, June 6, 2000.

Wine and Medical Practice, 4th ed. San Francisco: The Wine Institute, 1979.

AUTHOR'S BIOGRAPHY

Roman T. Solohub was born May 11, 1957, in England, but grew up in Chicago, Illinois. He graduated from Western Illinois University in 1979 with a B.S. While preparing for medical school, Roman decided to completely change course and joined the U.S. Navy to become an officer and naval aviator. He was commissioned as a naval officer in December 1981, and earned his U.S. Navy "wings of gold" in December 1982. As a patrol plane commander and mission commander flying the P3C Orion, the navy's "submarine hunter," Roman and his crew flew real world missions against our cold war opponents and represented our nation worldwide.

After leaving active duty in 1987 to fly for a major airline, Roman is currently a captain and instructor on the Boeing 767. He also stays busy giving motivational and corporate keynote speeches emphasizing responsible alcohol use.

Roman resides in Acworth, Georgia, with Jennifer, his wife of more than 25 years. They have two children: Christina, 23, a sophomore in law school, and Ryan, 21, a senior attending Florida State University.

INDEX

Give the Gift of

Clear Thinking
When Drinking

The Handbook for Responsible Alcohol Consumption

to Your Friends and Colleagues

CHECK YOUR LEADING BOOKSTORE OR ORDER HERE

❑ **YES**, I want _____ copies of *Clear Thinking When Drinking* at $15.00 each, plus $4.95 shipping per book (Georgia residents please add 90¢ sales tax per book). Canadian orders must be accompanied by a postal money order in U.S. funds. Allow 15 days for delivery.

❑ **YES**, I am interested in having Roman T. Solohub speak or give a seminar to my company, association, school, or organization. Please send information.

My check or money order for $_____ is enclosed.
Please charge my: ❑ Visa   ❑ MasterCard
                 ❑ Discover   ❑ American Express

Name _____

Organization _____

Address _____

City/State/Zip _____

Phone_____ Email _____

Card # _____

Exp. Date_____ Signature _____

Please make your check payable and return to:
Empennage Press
PO Box 801082 • Acworth, GA 30101
Call your credit card order to: 678-852-9659
or Fax to: 770-419-8008